The Winning Behaviours

The WINNING Behaviours

Generating Performance Through Leadership

DAVE ORMESHER

Book Guild Publishing
Sussex, England

First published in Great Britain in 2012 by
The Book Guild Ltd
Pavilion View
19 New Road
Brighton, BN1 1UF

Printed and bound in Spain under the supervision of
MRM Graphics Ltd, Winslow, Bucks.

A catalogue record for this book is available from
The British Library.

ISBN 978 1 84624 776 7

Contents

Foreword

Understanding leadership and winning behaviours, has been an evolution for us at Belron®. From the inception of our competency framework in 1999 it has been a relentless quest for greater understanding about the aspects of leadership that work, the ones which contribute most to our business goals. Dave describes the framework as 'concise yet comprehensive' but that phrase belies the hard work and thought that went into understanding the relationship between leadership behaviour and results, convincing us all and making it best practice.

Our approach has always been highly pragmatic; we invest in leadership because it is justified by the return. As CEO there's the added bonus that the winning behaviours create a culture where people enjoy performing to the best of their ability. In my opinion it makes Belron® a special place to work.

Not surprisingly there are many things I like about Dave's story but there are also some challenges. The fact that a leader's first set of data is generally a disappointment to them does not surprise me, I've seen it on enough development programs.

One of the reasons for this is that competency frameworks, and therefore development, focus exclusively on the positive aspects of leadership. Dave has identified the corrosive impact of what he describes as losing behaviours. He goes on to explain that research shows leaders to be not only blind to these losing behaviours they use, but also genuinely to believe they are actually using winning behaviours when they are not.

A key part of leadership development at Belron® is to play to your strengths and while that remains the ultimate goal it skips, for some, the key step of appreciating and overcoming losing behaviours that have a de-motivating impact on people around the leader. If you have losing behaviours in your leadership portfolio, which a third of us will in our first set of feedback, then the first challenge is to raise self-awareness of them and their impact.

The way Dave addresses both winning and losing behaviours balances this oversight in most competency frameworks, and this has been a new insight for me.

The year before Dave retired he asked, as part of the annual budget process, for funds to research and document the link between leadership and performance. The response from his colleagues demonstrates the commitment our organisation has to leadership as a strategic priority through his work: 'Who is disputing the link?'

I'm delighted Dave has captured in this book everything we learnt about leadership in Belron® and given us a few other things to think about. Whether you want to improve the impact of your personal leadership or get better results for your part of the business or the organisation itself, this book shares an approach which worked for us.

Gary Lubner
CEO, Belron®

Author's Note

The theories, hypotheses, opinions, judgements, conclusions, recommendations (and the like) contained in this book are those of the author only.

Belron® and the logo are registered trademarks of Belron® S.A. and its affiliated companies

Use of he/his/him in a general context throughout this book is for clarity and simplicity, and readers should assume that male or female is intended.

Acknowledgements

The winning behaviours framework and the book's content are based on real feedback gathered over many years together with my practical experience at Belron® both as a leader and as the individual responsible for leadership. I'm grateful to Belron® for providing access to a wealth of information on personal performance and of course to the people who provided insightful feedback.

I'd like to thank Gary for giving me firstly the opportunity and secondly the freedom to explore and develop our approach to leadership.

In particular I'd like to thank my sparring partner, Simon, who shared this journey with me. His challenge, support and friendship I genuinely appreciate.

For the last two years my wife, Michelle, could be forgiven for thinking I was still at work, on 'planet leadership' as she would describe it. Throughout, her encouragement and honest feedback have kept me on track. Thank you.

Finally to our son, Nick, who created all the illustrations in a style that perfectly complements the narrative.

Introduction

The winning behaviour framework is based on information gathered over ten years, from 2000 to 2010, on the behaviours associated with 'world class' executives in Belron®.

The Belron® context

Belron® is a global organisation providing a vehicle repair and replacement glazing service in thirty-three countries across five continents; indeed it is the world's largest. The markets served by Belron® represent 76 per cent of the world vehicle parc.

Whilst Belron® may not be a household name, it is home to some of the best known brands in the industry: Carglass® in continental Europe, Brazil and China; Safelite® in the United States; Autoglass® in the United Kingdom; and O'Brien® in Australia.

Belron® is a fast growing organisation that sees leadership as a strategic driver and fundamentally believes that effective leaders leverage discretionary performance from the people around them. Belron® operates 24/7 and completes a repair or replacement to a windscreen somewhere in the world every three seconds, generating annual sales in excess of two billion euros. Service delivery is widely dispersed, remote from both corporate and local head offices, which makes accountability and autonomy key. Delegating ruthlessly and with confidence would be a good way to describe the approach. Very little is controlled centrally; there's a belief that autonomous local business units understand their own markets far better than a corporate centre. However, the calibre of Belron® executives is considered so critical to the success of the organisation as to be an exception to that principle.

As a consequence, the corporate centre has a small number of Belron® wide priorities, leaving the business units in the countries wholly accountable for achieving their budget through the initiatives in their supporting operating plans, which are shared and agreed annually with the centre.

Throughout the period researched, Belron® focused on leadership as one of those central priorities. In practice this meant that an executive reporting to the chief executive officer, CEO, was specifically responsible for the leadership calibre of the executive group and the plans to improve it. There's a score to measure progress in both of the tools used to assess executives, so it was relatively easy to establish a composite organisational score as well as track individuals' develop-

Responsibilities are Clear

Role of the Centre	Role of the Business
✓ develop leadership talent	✓ understand the local market
✓ drive economies of scale	✓ deliver annual operating plans and achieve budget
✓ set global strategy and direction	✓ develop and maintain relationships with key influencers
✓ share best practice across the group	✓ deliver outstanding customer service
✓ grow and develop the group as a global business	✓ constantly improve operational efficiency
	✓ share and implement best practice

Fig 1 The responsibilities of the business units and the centre

ment. I was the person responsible for that composite score as well as delivering initiatives that would ensure the progress of the leadership calibre within Belron®.

The audience for this leadership KPI, key performance indicator, was the main board and their direct reports, the general managers and their local executive team. That represents two hundred individuals in total, a mixture of senior leadership in the corporate centre as well as in the thirty-three different countries.

The other central priorities common throughout the period were delivering the return the shareholders expected, geographical expansion and sharing best practice. I think that gives a strong indication of the importance of personal leadership to Belron®, partly in its own right because of the impact it has, but also in supporting delivery of the other strategic priorities.

The research

Belron® assesses executives in two ways. First, a Hay Group methodology is used that tracks leadership styles through to the organisational climate those styles create specifically for direct reports.[1] The definitions of styles and dimensions of climate are summarised in Appendix 1. Second is a more traditional and broader (beyond just direct reports) three hundred and sixty degree competency based review tool. Both feedback mechanisms provided quantitative feedback, as Belron® is an organisation that loves to have a score for the things that matter.

The competency based review tool explores all the dimensions of leadership, using a self-perspective as well as those of your boss, peers and direct reports (see Appendices 13 and 14).This contrasts with the Hay Group tool, which measures the climate experienced by direct reports only.

The competency based tool provided a wealth of qualitative data. The comments of over a thousand people giving feedback on just the leaders who were world class in specific competencies were collected. An analysis of these comments forms the basis for the book. The perspectives of those on the receiving end of outstanding leadership provide the best description of what winning behaviours look and feel like. The Belron® executive competency framework is summarised in Appendix 14.

Since both methods of assessment provide scores for leadership, I had the opportunity to focus only on the executives whose behaviour was regarded as truly outstanding rather than just leadership traits in general.

Belron® is a global organisation. As a consequence the research gathered is from a wide range of cultures, from business units at different stages in their development and in very different markets. In many ways it can be considered a corporate centre and thirty-three companies. The two feedback tools were, however, consistently applied because leadership is seen as a business priority.

A Global Organisation

Fig 2 A global organisation, with different markets and cultures

Feedback, the oxygen that sustains improved performance

Belron® is an organisation where individuals have become very comfortable sharing feedback. It's a great place to work if you appreciate the openness and desire to share insights to help you improve. If you are not predisposed to that approach,

I would imagine it's quite daunting. We'll see this frankness as much when we look at the losing behaviours as the winning ones. I'm grateful to all those who shared their views on leaders: they really bring winning behaviours alive and give us an aspiration for the kind of feedback we should aim for from those around us.

Losing behaviours, in contrast, are those associated with executives who left the organisation purely for performance reasons. They are as important as winning behaviours because, as we will see, they are certainly behaviours to avoid.

The best examples of feedback state what you see or hear followed by the impact that it has either on yourself, or on others. For example:

> *'One of my team was thrilled to get a call to*
> *congratulate him, it was very motivational.'*

> *'He can be too verbose and the key messages*
> *get lost as people switch off.'*

Best practice at Belron® was to run a feedback workshop with those contributing to a performance review in advance. A short session greatly improved the quality of the feedback, and that added insight improved the quality of the subsequent personal development plan.

Because so many of the examples were given in this format I was blessed with not just the behaviours that make the biggest difference but also a very clear view of the impact winning behaviours have on people around the leader. The impact on others is the link between personal leadership behaviour and an organisation's performance (Fig 3). It's an essential component of the model and is explored in Chapter 7.

The Belron® leadership philosophy

Belron® is an organisation that believes there is an output to leadership, a belief that developing leaders will improve business results. It's not seen as a 'nice to have'; more as a business essential. Competencies were first introduced in 1999 supported by a simple performance review. That was the last year Belron® failed to deliver its profit budget; in other words the investment was made as a business imperative. Having seen many competency frameworks, there's nothing in the content or definitions that makes them remarkable. I've summarised the Belron® competencies in Appendix 14; they include the competencies you'd expect to find in any large organisation.

The belief that there's a business critical output to leadership is reinforced by the fact that the CEO, Gary Lubner, made just one keynote address at the 2002 World Conference of Executives. It was not about customer service or business results but the need to recruit outstanding leaders. 'Management capability is the biggest constraint to profitable growth.' To grow profitably was the Belron® strategy throughout the period of research. Gary Lubner's view was that there are many attractive markets to enter and companies to acquire; those are not going to be an issue; the challenge is to have leaders throughout the organisation capable of leading their people through the changes that accompany rapid profitable growth.

He sums it up like this: 'If you put half a dozen business school graduates in a room together, they'd have the business model very quickly, so that's not going to differentiate us but I believe our leaders can.'

I was fortunate to work for Gary twice, earlier in my career when he was general manager of the UK business unit Autoglass® and latterly when I was the executive responsible for leadership in Belron®. We were reflecting on that when he observed: 'I always knew there was something that distinguished great from mediocre leaders when we worked at Autoglass® but I could not put my finger on it. The beauty about our approach now is that it's clear what those elements are, how they impact others and, as important, the bottom line. It now makes sense and gives people something to work on.'

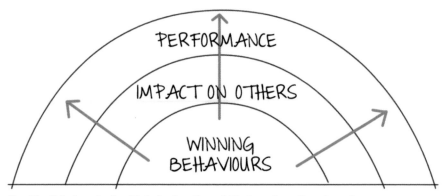

Fig 3 The links from leadership behaviour through the impact on others to performance

So what about the output to leadership, the business results?

From 2000 to 2010 Belron® grew profitably: sales by 12 per cent compound and profit by 18 per cent compound. Neither Belron® nor I believe that leadership was the only reason for such phenomenal and consistent growth (every year profit growth exceeded sales growth), particularly through the challenging years toward the end of that decade. A thorough knowledge of the business model for the industry and a constant focus on differentiating the organisation from its competitors, specifically through a superior customer service offer, were important. But a widely dispersed organisation where that service is delivered remotely requires world class leadership and the CEO realised that Belron® could leverage greater performance through a certain type of leadership. Unlike many things that impact the business, the quality of leadership demonstrated is completely within the control of Belron®. That explains why Belron® regards leadership as a central priority.

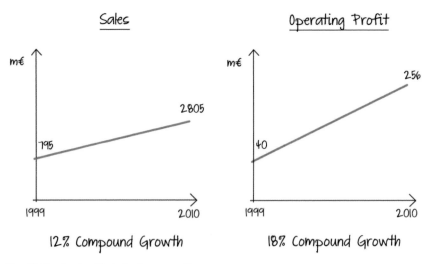

Fig 4 Linking leadership to business results

Part One

Generating Performance
Through Leadership

CHAPTER 1

Leadership Is Not Part Of Your Job
– It *Is* Your Job

How leadership behaviour can be traced through to an organisation's performance has been a fascination for me. Once you can demonstrate that link and understand how to develop leadership behaviour to have a more positive impact, what organisation would not want to make the investment and release the potential in their people?

I will demonstrate that leadership is not as complex as some purport it to be, that leadership is easy to measure and that, by knowing where to focus your leadership, capability will grow. As a result, you will have a positive impact on those around you as well as the performance of your organisation. My belief is that by the end of the book you will understand the elements of leadership behaviour better and feel encouraged to do something different. The three things to remember as we move through the book are that leadership behaviours, winning behaviours, have an impact on others that, in turn, drives results; it's as simple as that.

Fig 1.1 The links from leadership behaviour through the impact on others to performance

Before we start, I would like you to think about bosses and leaders you have seen or worked for and reflect on what the good and bad bosses actually did. How did that behaviour make you feel? We'll come back to your thoughts when we pull things together in the final chapter and consider whether winning behaviours have captured your own perspective on leadership. Just record what is 'top of mind' for you when you think about good and bad bosses you have experienced.

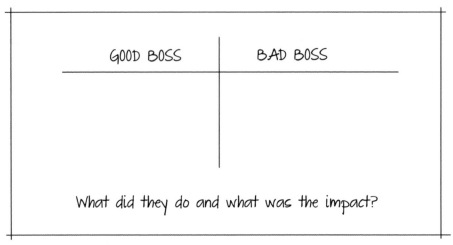

Fig 1.2 Good Boss, Bad Boss

Buying into the importance of leadership behaviour

Houldsworth and Machin state: 'work within Hay Group suggests that organisational climate [see Appendix 1] can directly account for up to thirty percent of
the variance in key performance business measures'.[1] You can take their word
for it, or look at the range of performance from teams in your company doing
the same thing, in a call centre for example. I'll wager the range of performance
reflects the Hay Group research, the reason being more to do with the qualities
of the leader than the ability of the followers. Alternatively, reflect on bosses you
have worked for yourself. Some you put in the extra effort at work; for others
you saved it for some other activity when you got home. We all wake up with a
tank full of energy to put into life; effective leaders encourage us to use that to
generate performance while we are at work. Your reflections on 'good boss, bad
boss' will no doubt support that argument.

The impact of personal leadership behaviours on performance is simply too big
to ignore. That's why an understanding of winning behaviours will transform your
ability as a leader and make a huge contribution to results through the people
around you. The impact of winning behaviours on others and the organisation
will be apparent to all.

From it's own anecdotes, Belron® quickly formed the view that leadership does
make a real difference; it is seen as an investment for which there's a return,
no different from investing in a marketing campaign or an acquisition in a new
country. We'll look at some of these examples in Appendices 12 and 19.

The view that leadership behaviours make a big difference is supported by

Goleman.[2] In considering the importance of IQ on success he suggests that it explains at most 10 per cent and as little as 4 per cent. In other words, it's a threshold competency.

McClelland's 1973 paper 'Testing for Competence rather than Intelligence' was amongst the first to suggest that a person's academic record is an unreliable predictor of success in a job and that competencies such as empathy and self-discipline are more likely to differentiate the successful.[3] He recommends an analysis of star performers in a role to establish precisely what those competencies are.

Buckingham and Coffman describe talents as 'recurring patterns of behaviour that can be productively applied,' suggesting that if you want a reliable predictor of success in a role you need to identify the talents for that role.[4] They go further in proposing that if you recruit on skills, knowledge and experience you will get a range of performance: 'only the presence of talents can explain why some succeed and others struggle'.[5]

Lots of sound advice but in practice recruiting for the 'right' behaviours is rare and it's rarer the higher the role is in the hierarchy. Goleman, in 'What Makes a Leader', argues that the right behaviours have a greater impact on whether a leader is successful.[6] 'Emotional intelligence proves to be twice as important for jobs at all levels. And it plays an increasingly important role at the highest levels of the company where differences in technical skills are of negligible importance.'

What's on a leader's CV is not enough

I believe that skills, knowledge and experience are not enough in an executive, that there are a set of behaviours that contribute to a leader being truly world class and that having leaders who behave in that way creates a culture that delivers outstanding results.

I'm not suggesting that having winning behaviours will compensate for a leader who is incompetent, lacking the relevant skills and without a track record of performance in similar roles. I'm proposing that it's the behaviours that differentiate outstanding from 'run of the mill' where leaders have identical skills, knowledge and experience. That's the competitive edge Belron® is seeking.

How Belron® approached this from an organisational perspective I've described in Chapter 9. Suffice to say for now that the whole of the recruitment, training, coaching and performance measurement agenda is built around the leadership behaviours that differentiate the outstanding from the mediocre.

Winning behaviours

From my research I've identified four winning behaviours and a cluster of losing behaviours to avoid. World class executives provide direction, they engage both around the task and the individual, they focus on performance and, as well as managing others, they manage themselves. That's it; couldn't be simpler.

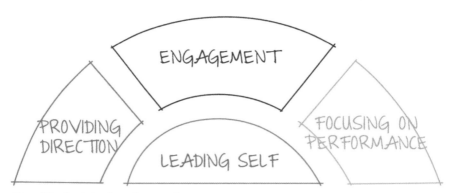

The Winning Behaviours

Fig 1.3 Winning behaviours framework

This is the combination of behaviours that has a very positive impact on those around the leader and drives business performance.

The structure of the book is to look at each of these in turn and also to analyse the losing behaviours. We'll then discover the impact of both winning and losing behaviours on others. In Chapter 8 we'll look at how to get started and how to put together a development plan. In Chapter 9 I'll describe the organisational approach to developing leadership capability. We'll bring it all together in Chapter 10. The appendices cover the data and research to support the winning behaviours framework. Appendix 20 also explains how to create your own diagnostic tool.

The book's style is to use the feedback gathered from those who experienced both world class and ineffective leadership to describe the behaviours, as in my opinion it's far better to use their words where possible rather than my own. I'll provide the opportunity to compare the winning behaviours framework against other leadership literature and will conclude each chapter with a diagnostic to help assess where you feel your relative strengths lie.

I have anchored the winning behaviours framework into traditional leadership reading, partly to demonstrate it's validity, but more importantly to offer alternative ways of looking at the same behaviours to improve understanding and prompt action.

The research is based exclusively on the views of those who actually experienced leadership themselves, the ones on the receiving end. Whilst the leaders' own views were available, a recurring theme throughout the feedback was the leaders' relatively poor self-awareness, indeed in some cases virtual blindness, as we will see. As a consequence I chose to exclude all self-views other than in assessing self-awareness in general.

I'm not suggesting that leaders don't know what they are doing. That's not true; there's invariably a business plan they are following. What I am saying is that the vast majority are blissfully unaware of the behaviours they are using to deliver the plan and how they are perceived by others, both positively and negatively.

Because other organisations use the Hay Group tool, it's clear that the Belron® executives started in exactly the same place as any other set of executives. As a group their first set of data is no different to the benchmark. You can see the evidence for this in Appendix 3. What differentiates Belron® from others is how each leader is encouraged by the organisation to respond.

So, there's more to leadership than just the skills, knowledge and experience you see on a CV or hear in an interview. Leadership behaviours make a huge difference and I would argue are more critical the higher in the organisation you are. Let's look at the winning behaviours in more detail.

Part Two

Winning Behaviours
And Their Impact

CHAPTER 2

A Guiding Star

'She takes the time to explain why it is so important; the vision is a bit like a guiding star. It inspires us and keeps us on course.'

Providing direction is leadership at its most basic level; without exception everyone wants to know what's expected of them and, even better, why. It's a good place for us to start, because when we move on to discuss engagement and a focus on performance the clarity achieved here will form a context for the behaviours associated with those clusters.

It's a recurring theme in leadership literature that knowing where the organisation is going and how people fit in is critical to performance. Kouses and Posner identify that inspiring a shared vision is a key leadership practice.[1] The leadership characteristics 'forward looking' and 'inspiring' have been a consistent response in answering the question 'What do people look for and admire in a leader?' in surveys since 1987.

The winning behaviour 'providing direction' can be broken down into six aspects, but in essence it's the clarity and confidence that comes when everyone is not only absolutely clear where the organisation is going, but also understands why it is so important. People appreciate how they, personally, will make a valuable contribution, but it goes beyond that to feeling a commitment to the imperative.

Where does the vision come from?

Providing direction starts with a vision, but where does that come from and what is it?

For most organisations and leaders the vision is there already, and invariably it is something that attracted the leader in the first place to the organisation. Collins describes 'good to great' companies as being more like hedgehogs 'that know one big thing and stick to it'.[2] He suggests that enduring companies retain their core purpose; it's the way they operate that adapts to a changing market. The implication is that the opportunity to create a new vision is rare, despite the fact that there is much literature on the subject, perhaps because it sounds like the type of thing leaders should be doing?

Before you decide a new vision is needed for your organisation, let me share two further perspectives to challenge your thinking.

Firstly, Kotter and Cohen describe eight sequential steps to implementing major change, of which only the third is 'Get the vision right.'[3] The first step is to 'Increase urgency.' It's a big mistake to contemplate new visions and strategy if there's no compelling reason to do so. It just won't work if no one can appreciate the need for a change in direction. If the literal equivalent of a burning platform is not experienced by the majority, if people are not yelling 'We've no choice; we need a new approach; it's a business imperative,' relook first at the existing vision.

Secondly, think about those who are committed to the existing priorities. Don't underestimate the emotional ties some may feel for what's in place already. LaFasto and Larson explain the difficulties in moving from one vision to another, most commonly the leader getting carried away with his own enthusiasm and leaving the rest behind.[4] The vital clarity around why the change is necessary is lost in the transition from one vision to another.

So, chances are that a vision is there already for you. My belief is that the issue for the majority of leaders is a lack of traction, urgency or desire to get there. The winning behaviours associated with providing clarity assume a vision is in place, a potentially inspirational 'hook'. The challenge is doing something with that vision, bringing it to life first for yourself and then for others. That's what the behaviours associated with providing direction achieve.

Let's define a vision as a compelling view of an ideal future state that appeals intrinsically to the people in that organisation. Whilst we talk about the ability to lead yourself in Chapter 5, it's worth emphasising here that a leader cannot demonstrate the behaviours or passion for the direction chosen unless they fundamentally believe in the vision themselves. Buckingham, when describing great leaders, explains this as a preoccupation with a better future that the leader constantly reflects on and refines until that image is absolutely clear in his own mind before he moves on to communicating with others to gain a shared inspiration.[5] Buckingham goes on to describe great leaders as people who 'transform our fear of the unknown into certainty of the future'.[6] Again, the emphasis is on clarity as an output that has a positive impact on others.

How is that clarity and confidence created through the six aspects to providing direction?

Leaders communicate frequently and consistently a clear sense of direction

The key words are 'frequently and consistently'. Leaders remind their teams of the importance of progress towards the vision at company meetings, team meetings and one-to-ones. They look for any and every opportunity to remind people why it is so important and recognise anything that helps take the organisation there. They do this through the agendas for meetings and the main topics of conversation with people.

> *'He never lets a conversation go by without some*
> *insightful observation on customer service.'*

It's hard to persuade people that customer service is an imperative if the first thing you ask about is something else or it's a late addition to the agenda. It just won't work. Indeed, it causes confusion, the opposite of clarity.

The most effective leaders when delivering keynote addresses will never waver from the vision itself and the small number of priorities that are making the biggest difference; and they make no apology for it. I'm sure there are times when they may be concerned that they sound repetitive, but that next address or conversation may well be the one where the light bulb goes on for someone. It's also reassuring for those in the audience to hear that the things they have been focusing on are the ones that are still having the biggest impact, that they are still making a valuable contribution.

> *'I am pleased to hear that his story does not change;*
> *I never get tired of hearing it.'*

Inspiring visions are never complicated; they are always short, simple and easily understood. Clarity comes from statements that require no explanation, and if they appeal to the heart and inspire, all the better. Some examples of feedback comments may bring this to life:

> *'She uses a simple device that everyone can relate to,*
> *from directors to the front line customer facing teams,*
> *even accounts receivable. It drives the*
> *business forward under one banner.'*

And linked to that leader's inner belief:

> *'The evidence of his understanding and passion*
> *is that he makes it simple for us to grasp.'*

Another important feature is that leaders link the big company-wide picture to what people actually do day to day. Lencioni suggests that one sign of a miserable job is irrelevance, the feeling that what you are doing doesn't matter to anyone.[7] The leader's job is to overcome this by helping people understand how they are contributing to something that is worthwhile, so that they feel valued.

The annual budget process, from creation to acceptance and sharing with your team, is a great opportunity to provide direction to people around you that gives you a chance to practise and improve every year.

Chris is a finance director; he's a seasoned veteran of several budget campaigns and, technically, probably the best in Group. As ever, Chris has been intimately involved in the process with the senior team from the beginning and knows the numbers inside out. He decides to give up three hours of his time to take his team through every slide the directors used in the budget presentation to Group and he even shares some of his supporting spreadsheets, which he's sure they will appreciate. But three months later in his performance review he receives feedback that his team lack clarity. He's had that kind of feedback before, which was why he scheduled time this year to share the full detail. 'How can that be? Why have they forgotten already?'

Chris knows he's missing something and decides to have a chat with one of his peers to see what they do. A couple of weeks later he meets up with Lou at a conference and they find a quiet corner for a coffee in the break. Lou took a different approach. Like Chris he had a meeting to discuss next year's budget. He reminded his team of the company vision and reassured them that it was not going to change. He gave a brief outline of all the initiatives that would contribute to achieving both the budget as well as progress towards the vision.

He then asked his team: 'So what do you think that means for us? Where do you think we fit in?' From the subsequent discussion there's an appreciation that the finance department can play a much broader role than monitoring and control. They agree to talk with the other departments, share their finance plans to support the budget and ask what they can do to support others. This leads to personal objectives that are linked to the 'bigger' company plans and to ongoing discussions about progress, with Lou in one-to-ones, with each other and with other departments throughout the year. As a consequence the agenda for Lou's team meetings is mainly around those personal objectives.

Both approaches take the same amount of time to share the budget. The tell style, which we'll explore in Chapter 6 in describing losing behaviours, does not get commitment because the agenda doesn't shift from Chris. His team will simply wait for the next set of instructions to follow to get their sense of direction, which has always been the way with Chris. He's not a 'bad' person; that's just how he is.

There are often 'givens' in the annual budget process. What Lou does is take advantage of what isn't given. He explains why some things are important and that the vision remains unchanged, and then encourages his team to discover for themselves how they can contribute to the big picture. Wherever possible he shifts to the team's agenda. The only reassurance Lou needs is that the actions do actually support the corporate goals, but it's unlikely they won't, using that approach. Lou's team know why the goal, objective and vision are so important to Lou and the organisation. Lou trusts them to choose the best route; I guess that's always been the way with Lou also.

Goleman describes these two alternative approaches to providing direction in the article 'Leadership that Gets Results'.[8] Chris's style he describes as coercive. 'It undermines one of the leader's prime tools – motivating them by showing them where their job fits into a grand shared vision. Such a loss, measured in terms of diminished clarity and commitment, leaves people alienated from their own jobs, wondering "How does any of this matter?" He describes Lou's style as authoritative. 'People who work for such leaders understand what they do matters and why [...] An authoritative leader states the end but generally gives people plenty of leeway to devise their own means.'

Lou's approach provides the opportunity to frequently and consistently communicate a clear sense of direction; it's not a one-off meeting at the beginning of the year with the box ticked. And building on Lencioni's point, he makes his team feel their job is relevant.

Finally it's not just the message but the way the vision is communicated. It gets through on two levels: what the leader says and the way he says it. There's something here about demonstrating enthusiasm but also being comfortable engaging in conversation about the vision. I think this sums it up:

> *'He'll show how excited he is, both verbally and physically,
> then he goes serious and explains why he is sold on
> the idea and how it fits into our overall strategy.'*

It's a mix of persuading through both logic and the heart that starts to build commitment.

Kouses and Posner's research reveals that another thing people look for in a leader is inspiration. Initially leaders rehearse and practise how they communicate the vision, trying to see it through the eyes of others, until through repetition and feedback they are comfortable that the passion they feel is transmitted. When the dialogue starts to come from the heart it's delivered with real conviction. Kouses and Posner recommend that you listen to yourself; if it doesn't fill you with enthusiasm it's unlikely to have that impact on others.[9]

Denning suggests that a vision is a particular type of story in which there's sufficient detail for it to be credible and become, through repetition, 'familiar terrain', but there's not the specific predictions that inevitably will prove wrong in the future.[10] He also recommends that an absence of a detailed path creates for the audience 'the mental space to create an analogous scenario for change in their own organisation', the empowerment we'll explore later. In sharing the vision, the trick is to convey a story that excites people but leaves them to refine the route as the future unfolds.

Communicating a Clear Sense of Direction

✔ FREQUENTLY

✔ CONSISTENTLY

✔ AS SIMPLY AS POSSIBLE

✔ HELPING PEOPLE SEE WHERE THEY FIT IN

✔ FOCUSING ON WHY, NOT WHAT

✔ SHOWING PERSONAL ENTHUSIASM

Fig 2.1 Communicating a clear sense of direction

Leaders focus on priorities

Covey sums this up as 'Put first things first.'[11] No matter what the temptation, the things that matter most should not be at the mercy of those things that, for example, leaders simply enjoy doing. Covey puts an interesting twist on the daily routine of looking at what is in your diary: 'The key is not to prioritise what is in your schedule but to schedule your priorities.'[12] That's what the following behaviours are all about.

If people engage emotionally with the vision it's the priorities that provide focus on the areas that will have the biggest impact. The Pareto concept applies here, that 20 per cent of activities are going to account for 80 per cent of the progress towards the vision. That is where precious resource in every form should be focused. The key is to have as small a number of priorities as possible – having too many is to have none. Of course, the few also need to be the right ones, but it's not difficult to do a simple impact/ease matrix to check you are focused on the right priorities.

Kaplan suggests the following questions will help: 'How often do I communicate a vision for my business?' 'Have I identified and communicated the three to five key priorities to achieve that vision?' 'If asked, would my people be able to articulate the vision and priorities?' and 'How am I spending my time? Does it match my key priorities?'[13]

Priorities themselves clearly come from an underlying belief in the direction being taken. The vision is often described as the leader's hobby horse – 'What else is there?' – and leaders assume the role of critical conscience when challenging 'flavours of the month' to check fit. They continually emphasise and acknowledge progress on the few things that are making the biggest difference.

People get a sense for the priorities because leaders ensure they are always given sufficient time for discussion in meetings. Leaders bring the focus of discussion back to the key issue by asking the right questions. You will see them recognise the views of others and then look for reassurance that those views are consistent with the end game. Those priorities become clear to others because of the way they are constantly highlighted in every interaction.

Leaders use the vision as a guide, a decision grid to assess proposals.

'Whilst she will never say no, you know that all projects are assessed for their strategic fit.'

They also ensure that the day-to-day distractions many succumb to do not get in the way of long-term progress. Focus on the key points is not lost in the plethora of projects.

Let me share Nicky's story.

Nicky, a call centre director, is under pressure. The good news is that the marketing campaign is successful and his inbound call centre is handling call volumes they have not experienced before. The bad news is that it's open plan and everyone in the building can see the level of abandoned calls. Even the general manager looks up at the statistics in bright lights every time there's a call of nature. This doesn't feel very comfortable for Nicky and it's not going to go away because the marketing department is like a child with a new toy.

To solve the problem, Nicky presents the case to his fellow directors to overflow calls to a third party. It's agreed, and he selects a provider to solve the problem. Well, certainly that problem is solved – abandoned calls are virtually eliminated – but his colleagues are still not happy. Conversion rates and customer satisfaction have fallen as calls are being handled by less experienced staff. Nicky has been distracted by a common day-to-day issue for a call centre director and lost sight of the priorities. It's easily done.

One way to avoid the detour is to stand back and ask, preferably with others, 'Are you sure we are tackling the right question?' Let's call it looking at different ways to frame the opportunity.[14] The Americans tackled the issue: 'How do I get a biro to work in space?' The Russians asked a different question: 'How do I write in space?' They found a pencil answered it rather than investing in the infamous 'space pen'. In Nicky's case, the question he should have been answering is 'How do I maximise conversion of inbound calls?'

Whilst it may be tempting as a leader to change priorities periodically, to show your initiative, the impact is invariably confusing so I would advise caution. Do so only when it is necessary and always take the time to explain why there's a need for a new priority. It's then worth considering whether there's a priority to drop.

Horovitz with Ohlsson-Corboz describe this focus as discipline, ensuring the

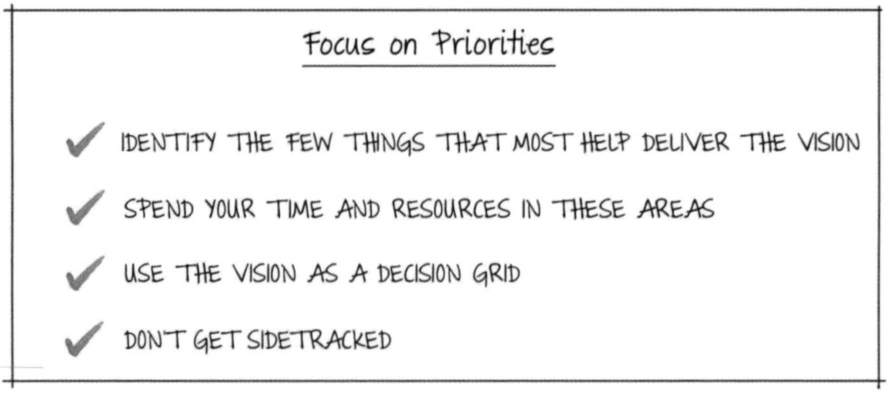

Focus on Priorities

✓ IDENTIFY THE FEW THINGS THAT MOST HELP DELIVER THE VISION

✓ SPEND YOUR TIME AND RESOURCES IN THESE AREAS

✓ USE THE VISION AS A DECISION GRID

✓ DON'T GET SIDETRACKED

Fig 2.2 Focus on priorities

company remains on its set course.[15] Ideally the priorities support each other and are obviously linked to the vision. It's also about the discipline of seeing something through to its conclusion. If trust (which requires people who want autonomy and leaders willing to delegate) is part of the way the company operates, they argue that the combination of discipline with trust speeds progress.

Sharing a vision and constantly demonstrating where the priorities lie is insufficient. We've got clarity, but what's needed next is some progress.

Leaders build commitment and encourage action towards a vision or strategy
Lencioni describes commitment as a function of clarity and buy-in.[16] So how can buy-in be added to the clarity established?

Leaders create the time to engage in dialogue to build commitment with their teams. Their approach is very inclusive; they appear open and supportive to new ways of moving ahead as long as they get the desired outcome.

> *'He is less worried about how we get there and more concerned about how we achieve the end goal.'*

Leaders involve the team in discussions on the best way to implement or make more rapid progress. They create positive energy in others through their empowering leadership style, which is reinforced through clear and consistent messages in every dialogue. Such people have an uncanny knack of being able to get into detail where others want it but when necessary stand back and look at the bigger picture, helping others who have become bogged down.

Returning to our example of the budget process, the early stages offer genuine opportunities to engage with your team, generate ideas and shape the operating plans to support the budget. What better way to build commitment to the final plan? The nuance is to gain commitment through involvement without relinquishing the leader's responsibility to ultimately deliver the vision.

Back to Nicky:

The lesson learnt about the importance of conversion rate on both business and customers has not been lost on Nicky. He's literally converted himself, and the focus on conversion rate has become, rightly, his raison d'être. Nicky is convinced that it is possible to raise conversion rate through more and better coaching and that this will have a huge impact on the company's growth strategy. But there's a problem: reducing team sizes, employing more team coaches and taking agents off the phone looks like a very costly initiative.

He discusses this with his team, who are equally convinced that coaching will make a big difference and indeed feel a personal commitment to that as a way forward. They agree that it would be unreasonable to expect the company to 'foot the bill' without commitment to a return. Nicky asks for ideas and they spend time looking at the potential to increase conversion and the related costs of doing so to confirm there's a good return. All the analysis is done by the team and they ask the finance department to check their assumptions.

At budget time the 'pitch' is to demonstrate the links between conversion and the company's goals and request the investment with the proviso that should it fail the old structure will be restored. Needless to say, with that level of commitment, it is a huge success and none of Nicky's team ever doubted it would be; it was their plan after all. And this time Nicky had his priorities right.

Leaders seek commitment from those with influence; they involve others in decision making to build ownership. Often this happens behind the scenes as lobbying. They are very good at gathering informal support through their network. You will see them engaging key people before decisions are made, often leaving ideas with people to give them time to reflect. Alternatively, they explore options with key players as a way to gain ownership.

Importantly, they build this commitment through one-to-ones with their own team. Effective questioning leads to a joint conclusion on fit with the bigger picture. That kind of curiosity comes naturally to leaders, who are always alert to ensure today's actions, effort and resources are linked to strategy. When someone comes up with a new idea you'll hear them saying: 'Just talk me through how that fits with our vision and priorities.'

Leaders are also willing to show their personal commitment, pinning their colours to the mast. They are often described as custodians or guardians of a cause and unwaveringly fly the flag for the things that matter. In particular, they show this by supporting longer-term investments in areas that are critical for delivery of the strategy, systems and training, for example. Again, they do this despite other short-term calls on valuable resource.

Commitment will not be achieved by simply communicating something new; it's a process that takes time.

Alex is a general manager who wants to bring together the various threads of a vision that have been in place for a long time in a way the whole organisation can embrace. Alex organises an 'away day', a well facilitated session away from the office where he and his team have the opportunity to get involved without the familiar distractions. Creating the right atmosphere, they have a highly productive day.

The vision is described as the circle of success. 'Only engaged and motivated employees will deliver the level of service our customers need to create the return our stakeholders require to reinvest in our people.' Nothing particularly clever about that, other than it's something that's very simple and easy to follow. Excited at capturing the vision, the directors are keen to launch this exciting revelation. To their dismay Alex suggests a different approach.

There's to be no big launch. However, all agendas will subsequently cover the three elements of business results, staff engagement and customer satisfaction. One-to-ones, the annual roadshow with employees, and the bonus scheme will reflect these and all future business cases for initiatives will consider their impact on the three elements. It took slightly longer to become part of the organisation's culture but it has become embedded and has stood the test of time for many years.

Building commitment to a vision requires far more than simply telling everyone.

Buckingham makes the same point, that followers shouldn't need to read the vision; they should see it in the way the leader acts.[17] That's what gives them confidence in the vision.

Some of that commitment comes from leaders who remain grounded in the practicality that visions must be delivered. They are happy to discuss practical issues of implementation, as concerned about what it will take as why it is so important.

As a result of the behaviours I've described, people feel the business is starting to build momentum in a direction; the vision is starting to get engrained in the organisation.

Denning argues that the most effective process of communication is first to grab the attention of the audience, second to stimulate action and finally to reinforce with reasons.[18] In other words, explain all the reasons why once the audience is ready to receive them. Explaining why is fundamental to this cluster of behaviours. People are far more likely to listen once they sense the urgency. Constantly reminding why gives people that added reassurance.

One final comment on commitment: it's critical for leaders to wish to encourage action, but the timing is key. You create frustration in others if you stimulate the desire to move heaven and earth only to announce it will happen some time next year. Other styles of communication or updates are possibly more appropriate in the meantime if action is not required in the foreseeable future.

In terms of providing direction, the leader's role is not, however, finished. There are further hoops to clear.

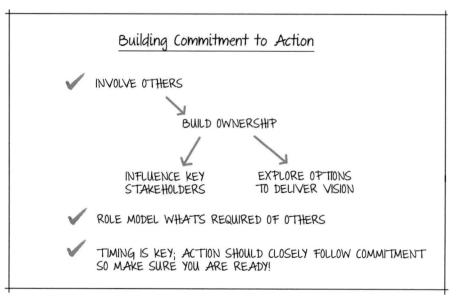

Fig 2.3 Building commitment to action

Leaders ensure alignment

Without alignment, clarity will become blurred, and people will see departments and functions appearing to move in slightly different directions and with different agendas. Alignment strengthens clarity and avoids confusion.

Leaders align first with strategy; they monitor the pulse of the organisation and take the time to reflect on how their efforts sit with where the business is going. They are sometimes referred to as 'company men', simply because their insights and subsequent actions ensure total alignment with company direction. It is usually attributed to clear and consistent communication. Alignment gives everybody confidence.

They also align with others, gaining buy-in through collaboration with groups and individuals. This focus on partnership greatly increases the chances of success. It's particularly critical between functions that jointly deliver service where customers are the first to see cracks. Leaders recognise the broader strategic nature of the challenges they take on and make a relentless effort to ensure complete alignment.

In one-to-ones you hear such leaders asking whether the impact on other departments and people has been considered. They also check how individual objectives and KPIs link to corporate ones. Further, their network will ensure that they pick up signals when there are inconsistencies.

Let me introduce Kim:

> As sales director, Kim is responsible for key accounts and has been working on a big player in the market for months. He's kept progress very much to himself because he doesn't want to 'count his chickens until they are hatched'. He's now concluded the deal. All the effort has been worth it because he's won the whole account rather than a share with competitors … and better still they want to move the volume straight away so impressed have they been with his offer and the relationship he's built. Naturally he agrees and can't wait to share the news at the next executive meeting.
>
> Kim is in for a shock, though, as both Nicky in the call centre and the recently appointed Sam in operations are aghast. They don't have the resources to cope; their own KPIs as well as service levels are going to suffer. Alex agrees and can't believe Kim has not considered how his promise will be delivered. Not a great start to the relationship with the newly won account as Kim has to go back and negotiate a phased transition.

It could all have been so different with the clarity and commitment that would come from greater alignment early in the process.

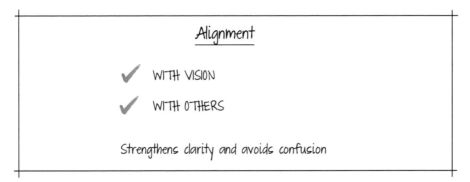

Fig 2.4 Alignment

Leaders demonstrate commercial insight, thinking quickly and analytically

Raw intelligence is greatly appreciated when used appropriately. This is one of those behaviours where there is a fine line between people seeing intellect used for the wider good as opposed to perceiving a degree of arrogance. Let's start with the positive aspects.

Speed of thinking is recognised positively when there's a purpose beyond the needs of leaders themselves; for example, when comprehensive analysis is used to keep the company a step ahead of the competition or when a quick evaluation of the seriousness of a threat is required. People appreciate a leader who helps them join up the dots, immediately sees the key drivers in their projects or spots the links to the organisation's strategy.

> 'He always seems to assess the situation quickly and put it within the framework of our strategy, I find that really helpful because it ensures we stay on course.'

It often involves spotting trends through being in touch with the market. Leaders appear to be 'tuned in' and to adapt their own model to take account of this, constantly refining their view. Leaders also take account of how economic changes will impact on both the market and the company. They use their intellect to see the big picture clearly.

This speed of thinking is so quick that others often see the insight as obvious after it has been integrated into the conversation. Leaders require skill and self-awareness to achieve that subtlety, which we'll explore in Chapter 5.

Leaders think broadly and are future oriented. In this sense they do not come across as parochial to others. They like to understand the wider context to maximise the chances of success. In taking a broader view they spot not only links but also inconsistencies between departments and initiatives. They are helpful in spotting interdependencies across functions, which encourages cooperation. Critically this supports the alignment behaviours.

Leaders make good use of intuition often in conjunction with their intellect. For example, they will ask to see figures if their instinct is not in line with the recommendation or they will dig deeper if it's not what they expect. There's a sense that the combination of intellect and intuition reduces risk.

Leonard and Swap propose that, when someone who is faced with a complex problem appears to come quickly not just to a solution but to a great one, it's more than just intellect.[19] They suggest that a wealth of previous experience contributes; because leaders have encountered a wide range of similar, if not the same, situations before such people sense the best action. They've discovered for themselves and stored away the combinations that are likely to work. Those watching attribute this to intuition. The rules of thumb that experience has taught people are seldom captured for others.

Leaders use numbers and data to influence and persuade.

'I don't know what comes first, a gut feel hypothesis that is then backed up by the data that supports the hypothesis or an analysis of the data to inform the view in the first place. Either way he puts a convincing case together which is very persuasive.'

They will make good use of expert opinion; sometimes it's their own reputation that is influential. In a positive sense they can be highly creative with numbers.

There is, however, a fine line where intellect can be perceived as corrosive rather than just negative. If used inappropriately it is seen as someone trying to demonstrate their own superior knowledge, which others find either intimidating or off-putting. It's perceived as overbearing and arrogant. It requires the behaviours I'll describe in leading self to optimise the use of intellect.

Belbin researched the impact of the mental ability of chairmen on the teams they led.[20] He looked at chairmen of average intelligence and those both above and below. He observed two types of behaviour from the 'not so clever' chairmen. Because of their inability to keep up with dialogue and debate issues they were perceived as out of touch or showing a lack of discipline around process. They appeared indecisive. He also observed the other extreme, with chairmen being overly concerned with making decisions quickly, perhaps based on simple majority at the expense of exploring options where they may have felt uncomfortable.

The 'clever' chairmen did no better. They appeared distracted by the excitement of complex problems. Their quick thinking meant they were constantly ahead of the others and again out of touch but for a different reason. They quickly saw flaws in the arguments of others but their own proposals were too complex for others to follow. In the extreme Belbin observed the team becoming a vehicle to satisfy the chairman's own strategy.

The chairmen with good average mental ability fared best, being on the same wavelength as most, which encouraged open discussion. When they saw someone with the talent to help through constructive criticism or appropriate suggestions

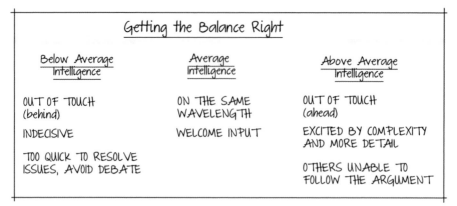

Fig 2.5 Intelligence: Getting the right balance

they welcomed it without seeing it as a threat to their authority.

We know that raw intelligence appropriately used is appreciated. Appropriate use comes with the ability to lead yourself, which we'll explore later. Let's assume leaders have this awareness; if so they can benefit a group in a number of ways. They can use their quick thinking to summarise the debate periodically, giving everyone the chance to get up to speed. They can use the mental space they have to check for people whose contribution has not been shared and encourage their view. In moving the discussion on they can look for ways to build on another's idea rather than, less sensitively, throwing even more proposals on a table that is already overflowing. Carnegie describes this as follows: 'If you are going to prove anything, don't let anyone know it, do it subtly. Be wiser than other people if you can but don't tell them so.'[21]

In Lencioni's 'The Five Temptations of a CEO', he refers to choosing 'certainty over clarity' as a temptation to avoid.[22] He suggests that executives spend too much time debating the finer points, believing that their analytical and financial acumen is what makes them great leaders rather than appreciating it has more to do with their behaviour. In wanting to demonstrate their commercial skill, they can get far too much into the detail; such need for precision hinders progress.

Goleman, Boyatzis and McKee quote Einstein: 'We should take care not to make the intellect our God. It has, of course, powerful muscles, but no personality. It cannot lead, it can only serve.'[23] They move on to explain that leaders need to engage emotionally with people as well. I think that sums it up nicely. Intellect is important and has its place, but without the other winning behaviours leadership is incomplete.

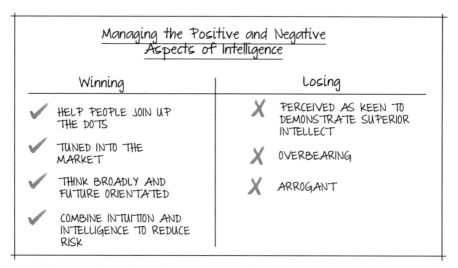

Managing the Positive and Negative Aspects of Intelligence

Winning	Losing
✓ HELP PEOPLE JOIN UP THE DOTS	✗ PERCEIVED AS KEEN TO DEMONSTRATE SUPERIOR INTELLECT
✓ TUNED INTO THE MARKET	✗ OVERBEARING
✓ THINK BROADLY AND FUTURE ORIENTATED	✗ ARROGANT
✓ COMBINE INTUITION AND INTELLIGENCE TO REDUCE RISK	

Fig 2.6 Managing the positive and negative aspects of intelligence

Leaders show a thirst for knowledge and insights

Sonnenfeld states that a quarter of CEOs believe their board members do not appreciate how complex and interconnected their business is.[24] It's impossible to align without those insights.

Leaders show a restless curiosity and seek to practically apply what they have learnt. They are interested in anything that will potentially add value, whether that's to improve their coaching skills or a new slant on a challenge they are facing. They enjoy digging to unearth evidence that will convince others. When a customer account is lost they are keen to explore what happened and learn from mistakes. They often read a lot, interpreting it and sharing it with their colleagues, seeking as wide a range of views and variety of biases as possible.

Leaders are keen to understand more about the business as a whole. There are no areas that don't get their attention. They seek insights not just from every aspect of the business but also from all levels. For such leaders an integral part of the conversation is: 'Where have you been? What did you learn? Who did you see?'

Thirst for knowledge goes hand in hand with the listening skills we'll talk about in the next chapter. Leaders see listening as a great investment of their time to help quench their thirst for knowledge.

Returning to Buckingham's description of great leaders, he recommends that a potential leader should be 'challenged to be more inquisitive, more curious and therefore more vivid in describing his image of a better future'.[25]

Charan describes leaders who spread their net widely to establish trends and then translate that into impact on the company.[26] He likens this to solving puzzles, a search for the missing pieces to the jigsaw. He suggests it requires 'an insatiable curiosity and interest in the world and an intense drive to find out what you do not know'. They constantly drill for more information and adjust their business models or thinking as more data is unearthed.

Collins describes the first stage of corporate decline as 'hubris born of success'.[27] A symptom is that leaders have lost the thirst for knowledge and the insights that previously made them great.

Showing a Thirst for Insights

- ✔ NATURALLY CURIOUS
- ✔ INTERESTED IN ANYTHING THAT ADDS VALUE
- ✔ LEARNING FROM MISTAKES
- ✔ SEEKING INFORMATION BROADLY AND ON ALL LEVELS

Fig 2.7 Showing a thirst for insights

To summarise, there's much more to providing direction than having a vision; it's the associated behaviours that breathe life into it through others. It is, however, worth remembering that a compelling vision underpins it all. Offermann describes how leaders can be misled by followers and recommends that to avoid this they should 'keep vision and value front and centre. It's much easier to get sidetracked when you are unclear about what the main track is.'[28] That's good advice; let your vision be your guiding star.

LaFasto and Larson suggest that clarity drives confidence and that confidence drives commitment.[29] That's exactly what we are looking for from this cluster of behaviours, a clarity that gives people confidence in the direction provided and the commitment to engage and act.

Not surprisingly, the biggest impact of this cluster of behaviours on others is clarity. Clarity is the single most important driver of performance. Can you imagine working in a place where it's unclear what your role is, where you fit in, what's expected of you, and where that organisation is going? As Lencioni remarks, feeling irrelevant is miserable and highly de-motivating.[30] The winning behaviours associated with providing direction guarantee that clarity.

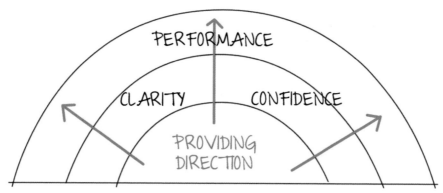

Fig 2.8 Links from providing direction through impact on others to performance

The following questions will help you assess your strengths relative to the behaviours associated with providing direction. Your own view is interesting but I'm sure it would be more insightful to get perceptions from other groups, your boss, your team and your peers to compare with your own. Are you achieving clarity, gaining commitment and instilling confidence through these behaviours?

How Characteristic are the Following for the Leader being Evaluated?

PROVIDING DIRECTION

	NOT AT ALL		SOMEWHAT		VERY	DON'T KNOW
COMMUNICATES FREQUENTLY AND CONSISTENTLY A CLEAR SENSE OF DIRECTION	☐	☐	☐	☐	☐	☐
FOCUSES ON PRIORITIES	☐	☐	☐	☐	☐	☐
BUILDS COMMITMENT AND ENCOURAGES ACTION TOWARDS A VISION OR STRATEGY	☐	☐	☐	☐	☐	☐
ENSURES ALIGNMENT BOTH WITH OTHERS AND ORGANISATIONAL STRATEGY	☐	☐	☐	☐	☐	☐
DEMONSTRATES COMMERCIAL INSIGHT THINKS QUICKLY AND ANALYTICALLY	☐	☐	☐	☐	☐	☐
SHOWS A THIRST FOR KNOWLEDGE AND INSIGHTS	☐	☐	☐	☐	☐	☐

CHAPTER 3

Where I Belong

'He really believes in team work. We see his face light up when we achieve things together and he's always there when I need him. It makes me feel really good to be here.'

Engagement is the second winning behaviour and we'll explore it on two levels: with individuals and around tasks. Research by Gratton and Erickson found that 'the most productive, innovative teams were typically led by people who were both task and relationship oriented'.[1] Their analysis was that leaders engage first around the task, to get things going, and then focus on relationships to manage the team dynamics.

Lencioni describes anonymity as being invisible.[2] You can't possibly feel motivated if no one knows you, let alone understands you. At its basic level, forgetting or failing to call someone by their name, which is a very precious thing to them, is anonymity.

There's a consistent theme that runs throughout the cluster of behaviours associated with engagement and that's listening. It's inconceivable that a leader will excel in this area unless he is a good listener; and such people are relatively rare. Whilst the communication skills of speech and writing are developed at school and presentation skills courses are available later in life, listening skills are largely overlooked. Yet when you meet someone who genuinely listens and everything appears to be focused on you, the impact is profound.

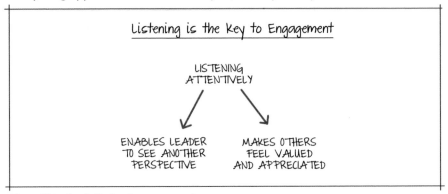

Fig 3.1 Listening is the key to engagement

Leaders listen attentively

Leaders demonstrate attention physically through a combination of eye contact and body language. They find the balance between proximity and providing space. Leaders never appear distracted when in discussion. But it goes beyond that: they are inclusive, interested in hearing other people's views and sensitive to the feelings they express. This interest and compassion leaves people feeling the leader is there 100 per cent for them.

Because the mind thinks quicker than someone else talks, people in a hurry tend to second-guess how a speaker will finish the sentence; their mind drifts to their own reply or a smart riposte. That's not listening on a level of genuine interest. Attentive listening is characterised by periods of silence, where the leader listens to everything and reflects before choosing the most appropriate response. Some describe this as not jumping to conclusions, instead listening before talking to gauge the mood or feelings around the situation.

One way to judge listening skills is by the quality of the answer or the next question. Listening is about giving someone else the opportunity to shape and share their thoughts, feelings and ideas. It's a very unselfish act.

By listening attentively and responding thoughtfully, leaders demonstrate they have understood and given due consideration. It's that behaviour from a leader that makes people feel they are valued and appreciated. People just feel comfortable talking with someone who has those qualities. Not surprisingly, it encourages even more input and, whilst agreement is not necessarily a precondition of listening, what does happen is that people feel they have been heard. That's very important to them.

In a partnership where a leader is seeking 'win–win' a combination of acute listening skills and the mental rigour to take the time to reflect, assess and review the new information gathered is critical. Otherwise why ask in the first place? It just leaves a feeling of disrespect if all you are doing is making things fit to your preconceived notion and playing them back to your so-called 'partner'.

Sharing airtime is another great indicator of listening skills, although self-awareness of this is often poor, because we are preoccupied with our own thoughts and for a variety of reasons wish to share them. It is, however, perfectly clear to others when a leader manages their share of voice, and welcomed.

'He is not domineering or hogging the conversation; he's happy to let me finish what I want to say and actively encourages me to do so.'

Fran is head of HR; he's a social character, gregarious and the life and soul of the party. Fran has just received feedback in his performance review that is a complete shock to him. There's a recurring theme to which he is completely blind.

On providing direction:
'Fran talks so much that it is hard to find the information that is relevant. Sometimes I just switch off and hope I don't miss anything important.'

'He talks about so many things I become unclear where my priorities lie.'

On **engagement**:
'Amazing! Fran wasn't even invited to the meeting but talked non-stop for most of it.'

'Only his agenda really; have to fight to get your points on the list because he talks so much, then he'll just say he's run out of time and has to go.'

'When I see Fran's name on the mobile I just send it to voicemail. I don't have the time for another disjointed monologue, I'm really sorry.'

On focus on performance:
'It's a bit like a teacher–student relationship; he comes with loads of ideas to try but then I just want to be left to get on with it rather than constantly chased for an update.'

On leading self:
'Fran acknowledges his verboseness but seems unable to control it, especially when it's one of his pet topics. He can't help himself.'

Fran didn't recognise any of the comments, and challenged whether they were accurate. He'd thought he was liked by everyone, so how could they say such things and in his performance review as well?

His boss Alex suggested he take time to reflect and reread the feedback. Next time they met Fran had calmed down a lot but was still finding it difficult to believe what he was reading. Alex agreed that progress was unlikely whilst Fran still did not appreciate his share of airtime. He asked Fran if he could attend his next team meeting as a guest; he'd do an update on company-wide initiatives and stay under the auspices of being interested but really observe and experience Fran's airtime. He asked Fran to behave as normal. In a meeting of nine people Fran talked over half the time.

Chatting with Alex later Fran made a commitment that his personal development plan would focus exclusively on his share of airtime without reducing his effectiveness as a leader. He joked, 'But what will I do with the rest of the time?' Alex joked in response, 'You could try listening.' The point was not lost on Fran.

It's a surprisingly common story and raises a number of issues. A large share of voice impacts negatively across the complete range of leadership behaviours and not just engagement. It's not unusual to find that everyone is aware of the behaviour and impact except the leader. You can imagine the talk in the corridor after meetings: 'How does he talk for so long; you'd think he'd get hoarse' and 'I see Fran was his usual self today; you'd think someone would tell him.' But, despite everyone knowing, no one tells Fran. So Fran doesn't know and as a result continues with the behaviour, which in the absence of feedback he feels is working. Why would he do anything different?

It's feedback that moves a blind spot into the public domain, but there are lots of emotions attached to the giving and receiving of feedback that many choose to avoid and leave to someone else. There's a way to encourage yourself to overcome the emotions associated with revealing a blind spot to someone. If you are aware of the behaviour and the impact it has, but choose to say nothing, what does that make you? Ask yourself: are you comfortable with that, especially if they are a team mate? Surely it's a genuine gesture to share honest feedback? Why leave a colleague blind to what you see?

There's a pattern to receiving feedback that everyone goes through; the only thing that varies is how long it takes. First there's denial (that's not me) then there's anger (how could they?) before finally there's acceptance (I believe they are right). When we look at focusing on performance in Chapter 4, the role of leaders is firstly to work through those phases themselves and secondly to help their teams do the same.

What's interesting is that a combination of reducing airtime and developing listening skills, both basic leadership behaviours, has an immediate impact on others, unlike plans to change other aspects of behaviour where opportunities to demonstrate a new approach come less frequently. Fran can, and did, start practising straight away.

Carnegie paints a less favourable picture, describing people who talk over others and refuse to listen as '[b]ores intoxicated with their own egos, drunk with a sense of their own importance'.[3]

By listening attentively leaders will pick up what makes an organisation tick – who, irrespective of hierarchy, has influence – and discover the crucial social networks. In this way leaders build a political awareness of the organisation.

Covey's instructions for listening are: 'Seek first to understand and then to be understood.'[4] If leaders approach others with that in mind they will 'get inside another person's frame of reference'.

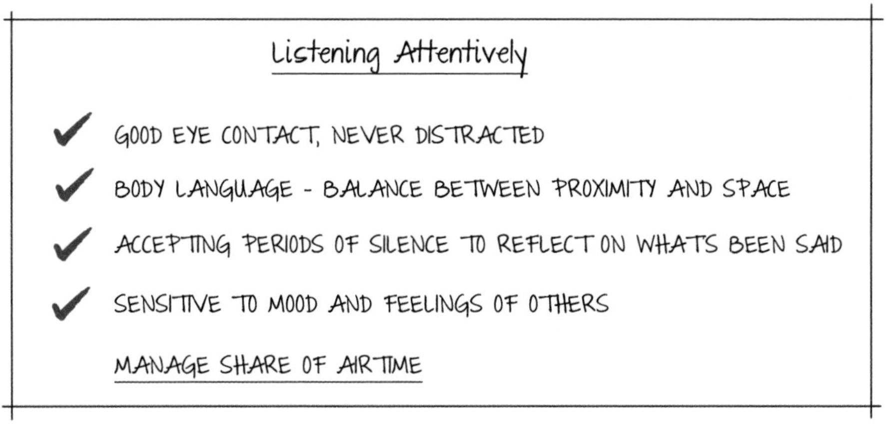

Listening Attentively

✔ GOOD EYE CONTACT, NEVER DISTRACTED

✔ BODY LANGUAGE - BALANCE BETWEEN PROXIMITY AND SPACE

✔ ACCEPTING PERIODS OF SILENCE TO REFLECT ON WHATS BEEN SAID

✔ SENSITIVE TO MOOD AND FEELINGS OF OTHERS

MANAGE SHARE OF AIRTIME

Fig 3.2 Listening attentively

Leaders show consideration

Carnegie proposes 'don't criticise, condemn or complain' as one of three principles for handling people.[5] He suggests that there is enjoyment and insight to be gained from finding out why people are the way they are. It 'breeds tolerance and kindness', and understanding people is far more profitable than criticising them. Another principle is to 'arouse in others an eager want', which requires leaders to understand completely other people's points of view, seeing things from their perspective as much as the leaders' own.

Leaders show consideration for the feelings of others. They ask questions but appear to be looking for what is not said as much as what is. When communicating decisions that will impact the feelings of others they are particularly sensitive, taking time to think through the best way to handle the situation and always appearing to keep their options open to the last minute to build in new nuances they sense.

You notice this consideration when leaders are facilitating; their attention is as much on the audience as on the content. The audience get the feeling that the session is for them rather than an opportunity for a leader to impress with what they know.

As with attentive listening, consideration for the feelings of others encourages them to share more of themselves.

> 'He's a great colleague; I feel very comfortable sharing even areas of vulnerability. This is because I believe he has the ability to get into my shoes and see things from my perspective.'

The Johari window, named after its creators Joseph Luft and Harry Ingham, is a very simple model that helps understand interactions between people.[6] The four window panes, described as open, hidden, blind and unknown, represent different types of personal awareness.

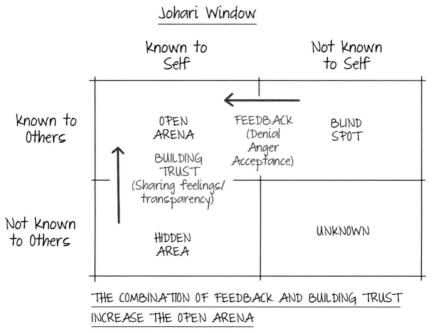

Fig 3.3 Johari window

In the Johari window high performance leaders increase the size of their open arena by seeking feedback to reduce the blind spot. We'll look at this in more detail when we focus on performance. But what's relevant to engagement is that, through building trust, individuals share more of their hidden area, moving it into the open arena. Two behaviours help: considering others' feelings and displaying trust and transparency, which we'll explore later in this chapter. Both of these encourage sharing.

The Johari window is a very simple device but a great way to build leadership effectiveness. You simply think about how to make your open arena bigger. The process of moving the hidden into the open is called self-disclosure and it's often associated with reciprocal behaviour. As I share more about myself, others share information about themselves that was previously hidden to me. O'Toole and Bennis describe trust as a symbiotic relationship: 'leaders must first trust others before others will trust them'.[7]

Leaders show consideration not only for the feelings of others but also for their needs. Sometimes this is described as interpersonal skills. Leaders show great understanding of the challenges faced by other people or groups. They are alert in conversation to the interests and motivations of other parties to help work towards the best outcome for all.

Leaders show empathy but not necessarily sympathy. In showing consideration they put themselves in others' shoes, seeing things through their paradigm of life, with the reality of each other person's heart and logic.

Leaders show consideration without compromising. They challenge hard, speak their mind without dominating the discussion and encourage alternative opinions but always with an eye and ear for their colleagues' feelings. They deal with issues about personal behaviour firmly and sensitively. Leaders are keen to resolve issues immediately that may prevent future cooperation rather than ignore them.

They don't lose sight of their own priorities whilst being sensitive to the needs of others. Consideration is shown in achieving both.

Finally, leaders demonstrate this behaviour with everyone; they relate with people on a personal level, no matter where they sit in the organisational hierarchy. They are warm people, fun to work with, and they understand the differences between characters and cultures well, so consequently they can have an impact on both.

A common way that leaders demonstrate lack of consideration for others is simply turning up late for meetings. They are best described as 'time bandits' and, if you wish to measure the size of their haul, simply multiply the number of minutes they are late by the number of people sitting waiting. It usually represents a lot of unproductive time.

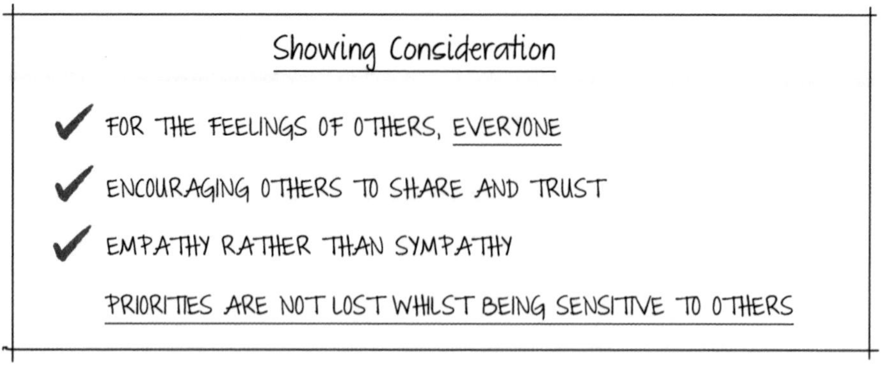

Showing Consideration

✔ FOR THE FEELINGS OF OTHERS, EVERYONE

✔ ENCOURAGING OTHERS TO SHARE AND TRUST

✔ EMPATHY RATHER THAN SYMPATHY

PRIORITIES ARE NOT LOST WHILST BEING SENSITIVE TO OTHERS

Fig 3.4 Showing consideration

Leaders seek and consider the views and opinions of others

Not only are leaders considerate but they also consider others' views.

Some leaders are only interested in the views of certain people. You've got a quality issue with your product or service, everyone in the front line is aware of it and moans to management at every opportunity, but nothing gets done until a paid consultant comes in. Leaders listen to consultants' opinions because they pay for them but normal service would be resumed much earlier, at significantly less cost, if they listened to people motivated by the fact that their boss is interested in their views. And where do you think consultants' opinions come from anyway?! Cialdini attributes this to the principle of authority, the idea that people defer to experts.[8] I'm suggesting that it's worth reflecting who the experts really are. Leaders spread their nets as wide as possible and are always alert, irrespective of who they're talking to.

Leaders seek opinion to help form their own views, being happy to use many different touch points to develop an opinion. Those conversations also give an indication of the impact the decision will have on other parties. It helps leaders shape how to deliver the message whilst demonstrating consideration. Conversations with them are more 'I'm thinking of ... what do you think?' than 'I've decided and am just letting you know.'

Constantly seeking advice and opinion helps leaders refine their thinking and identify new opportunities. Where there is doubt, leaders are comfortable bouncing ideas around without relinquishing their responsibilities. This kind of involvement has a positive impact on teams and intriguingly builds confidence in the leader.

Leaders listen to options and alternatives to strengthen bonds with people. They achieve this because the people involved feel their own thoughts are valued, particularly if the leader is seen to seriously consider them or does something with the input. Asking for input strengthens the bond, especially when team decisions are made as a group. It's not just the act of asking and listening that builds this bond; there's a perceived emotional attachment that goes with it.

> '*High levels of empathy make him a great person to be around. Whilst he won't always agree with me, he'll always see my point of view, which makes the conversation so engaging.*'

Knowing the views and feelings of others is also critical to managing change. Leaders can't communicate to allay fears if they are unsure what those fears are in the first place.

Considering the views of others ensures that better decisions are made. A team environment where opinions are exchanged optimises both the quality of the discussion and the quality of the output. The behaviours such leaders show are having an open door, being keen to initiate full and frank debates, and welcoming challenges, as well as demonstrating a genuine desire to listen to other views and consider them alongside their own.

This behaviour is vital when negotiating, as Sebenius, in 'Six Habits of Merely Effective Negotiators', points out.[9] It's important not to neglect the other side's problem. They have their own reasons that you need to ascertain and explore. It's a statement of the obvious but none the less true: if you want to change someone's mind you must first learn where that person's mind is. To quote Carnegie, 'If there is any one secret to success, it lies in the ability to get the other person's point of view and see things from that person's angle as well as from your own.'[10] Sebenius suggests that the more adversarial the relationship, the more difficult this becomes.[11] Combining that with what's called a self-serving bias (interpreting things favourably from your own perspective) is a big challenge when leaders start to feel the pressure to act or make a decision.

Asking the views of people is one thing; seriously considering them is another. Our judgement is skewed by this self-serving bias. We tend to give greater weight to views and opinions that support our own outlook or model. That's why to consider as well as to seek the opinions of another is so challenging.

Kline describes equality as a component of a thinking environment. It involves regarding each other as 'thinking peers'. Knowing you will have the time to talk improves the quality of your listening instead of causing you to focus on when and how to interject. 'To be interrupted is not good. To get lucky and not be interrupted is better. But to know you are not going to be interrupted, that is categorically different. That is bliss. The fact that the person can relax in the knowledge that you are not going to take over, talk, interrupt, manoeuvre or manipulate is one of the key reasons they can think so well around you.'[12] Kline also suggests that leaders should role-model that permission is not required to share facts or truth or express feelings.[13]

Can you recall a poor decision being made after a healthy debate with a frank exchange of views?

If you believe you are someone who spends time thinking about things from other people's points of view, try for a moment to contrast your interest in yourself and your own needs with the time you actually spend considering others. And when you've concluded, reflect that most people will be like you.

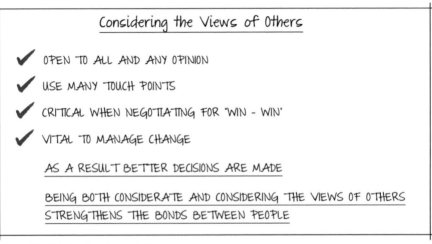

Fig 3.5 Considering the views of others

Leaders invest time to create and maintain networks

It's now time to apply the behaviours of attentive listening while both considering the views of and being considerate of others.

Leaders spread themselves widely and at all levels. They demonstrate the ability to walk with kings whilst keeping the common touch. Their extensive lists of contacts, both inside and outside the organisation, are testimony to a highly collaborative nature. Leaders not only do this themselves but actively encourage their teams to do likewise. Some leaders take advantage of that secondary network to further their knowledge and insights when catching up with their team.

You'll see it at conferences or meetings: some leaders are constantly on the look-out for new contacts, more information or other perspectives. Coffee breaks are a great time to sow for a future harvest. Leaders love being around people but with the added bonus of using whatever they learn. And because they are skilled in asking the right questions and listening intently they learn a great deal.

Leaders use their network to develop their own strategic thinking or to bring external perspectives, for example, about competitors, into team meetings. Networks are also an opportunity to influence key players either directly or through word of mouth. The point is that a wide network serves a broader purpose perhaps as well as intrinsically satisfying the leader's desire to be with people. For some people it's just natural.

Gratton and Erickson describe many ways of building a social network, such as mentoring and coaching beyond corporate boundaries and taking second-ments or project work in different parts of the business as part of a career plan.[14] Induction programmes for new recruits offer opportunities not just to add to a leader's network but to seek some current external experience and add to the leader's library of knowledge and potential contacts. Helping a new person put together an induction plan is a good way to get them started on their own internal network. Gratton and Erickson suggest that mentoring and coaching beyond a leader's own 'patch' are part of the culture that builds an ethic of collaboration as well as extending a social network. Collaborative behaviour is another aspect of engagement we'll look at shortly.

Gladwell, in 'The Tipping Point', shares an early example from 1775 of not just social networking but also the value such behaviours can bring.[15] He describes how Paul Revere's message that the British were advancing was received yet William Dawes carrying the same message failed to get through. Gladwell describes Revere as a connector – someone who knows lots of people and, because they engage in a wide range of activities, can act as a link between diverse social circles. They like everyone, they are social animals and they don't consciously filter who they will engage with.

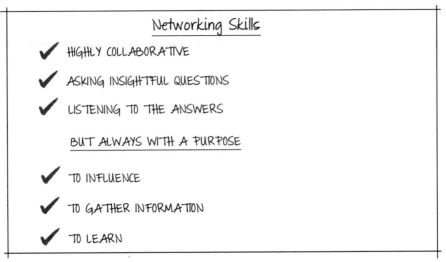

Fig 3.6 Networking skills

Leaders share relevant information and keep people updated

Whether they are well networked or widely read, leaders interpret what they have learnt and share with their colleagues anything that is relevant. People rely heavily on this; they appreciate the quality of the information and the leader develops a reputation for the calibre of his sources, which encourages them further. Others appreciate that a leader makes an effort to share with them anything that could affect their work.

It seems obvious, but starving teams of information that enables them to do their jobs properly is often, sadly, overlooked, even if the information is not withheld deliberately. It's a common criticism of leaders. Sharing information on a 'need to know' basis undermines the trust element of engagement. Being open with information is a basis for both an organisation's culture and its effectiveness. Discomfort at the thought of sharing potentially sensitive information is invariably offset by the positive impact it has on others and on the quality of their decisions.

Linked with the desire to be considerate, leaders are sensitive about what information they share. If they do not divulge all the details it is because they have thought through the implications. When a leader moves on to a new role, the ultimate act of sharing is to pass on graciously the knowledge and passion for the topic to his successor as part of their induction.

Leaders share progress on broader strategy to reassure people that the initiatives undertaken locally remain aligned with the company. In a similar fashion they encourage their teams to update on their own projects, partly for alignment but also as an opportunity to generate debate and new perspectives.

Failure to share information creates one of two reactions: either frustration, because vital data withheld is perceived as necessary to do the job; or confusion, as followers 'fill in the blanks' for themselves, usually with different and conflicting interpretations.

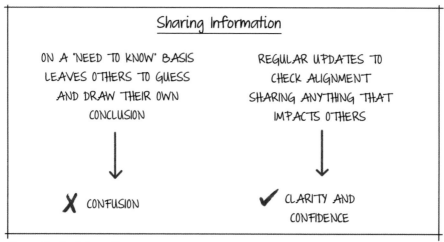

Fig 3.7 Sharing information

Leaders work collaboratively with others; they are team workers

'The teams he leads or is a part of are fun,
hard working and achievement oriented.'

Teams work best with a combination of enjoyment and engagement alongside properly focused tasks with the team dividend of more stretching targets through better solutions.

Genuinely seeking greater involvement is the foundation for collaboration. It comes from a belief that several minds will craft a better solution than one. It builds on the behaviours we've already discussed in engagement: being naturally inclusive, valuing the input of others and being comfortable with the cut and thrust of debate. And there is something else: not only is there a better solution but there is personal commitment to that decision as well. When the discussion is concluded, the whole team speaks with one voice. Involvement in the process and the fact that leaders will go to great lengths to ensure everyone's view is heard creates a real boost in terms of team spirit.

Leaders actively contribute to building strong team dynamics. They are anxious to play their part in developing a consensus that will work well for the team by building positive relationships with others and taking steps to resolve conflicts that arise. They role-model team behaviours; if they see a lack of cooperation they don't complain to others or moan, but look for ways to get involved themselves or influence through their network. Team players are invariably seen as both supportive and challenging; they seem to get the balance just right. This was a recurring theme to the feedback on world class leaders. These words are often used together when giving feedback on outstanding leaders. They tend to keep politics out of meetings because they know it undermines team work; it cramps dialogue rather than releasing the potential of collaboration.

Supportive behaviour is not the same as passive behaviour, going with the flow and not rustling anyone's feathers. Supportive behaviour is helping overcome constraints, encouraging a colleague to finish sharing their point of view and working to avoid the misinterpretation of an opinion, defending where necessary.

Challenging behaviour is usually very productive: it leads to issues being resolved rather than being shelved for another day. As a generalisation we make up our minds and form a view quickly; we are then relatively slow to change once emotionally or logically we have 'bought into it'. Constructive challenge, as opposed to critical challenge, enables this process to be more fluid and views to become less entrenched.

At the other extreme to challenging behaviour is 'group think', where people either don't know how to disagree or simply don't want to. Offermann attributes this pressure to conform to what psychologists call 'cognitive misers', people choosing the shortcut of automatically agreeing rather than debate.[16] She states that 'whilst leaders pride themselves on their willingness to take unpopular stands, most prefer conformity to controversy'.

Lencioni describes the need to avoid choosing harmony over productive conflict.[17] A leader who attempts to gloss over conflict in meetings simply sends the wrong message. Leaders, he argues, should encourage 'tolerant discord', as feeling free to air views with enthusiasm avoids 'stifling important interchanges of ideas'.

Collins makes a similar point in 'Good to Great' that there's a level beyond just letting people have their say and voice their opinion. 'When the truth is heard and facts confronted, better decisions are made.'[18]

Leaders never put their needs above those of the team; they show great loyalty. Commonly looking for win–win outcomes, they are willing to compromise or forgo something if it is for the good of the business or the team. They put team interests ahead of personal goals, perhaps by volunteering to take responsibility for the work others do not want. When a decision is made they are totally committed to doing whatever is required. Loyalty to the team is one of the things that attracts people to leaders. Its presence matters a great deal to those invited to work with a team. They are described as 'team men' because they want to take decisions together, respecting and valuing everyone's input and staying absolutely committed to team decisions.

LaFasto and Larson attribute the following behaviours to a collaborative climate: leaders remove barriers to open dialogue and talk about the tough issues they feel are on others' minds.[19] They also argue there's an absence of trust in leaders at both ends of the 'control over decisions spectrum', whether that's micromanaging or at the other extreme no desire to influence, abdication.[20]

> The senior leadership team are struggling. They have a significant project to work on but whilst the issue is clear there appears to be a range of views on how to tackle it. They are following a process familiar to them all except Sam, who is new to the organisation. It's called the ICE model: idea generation, gathering ideas through a variety of approaches; creation, funnelling ideas and investing in a few; through to execution, planning to deliver the selected option.[21]

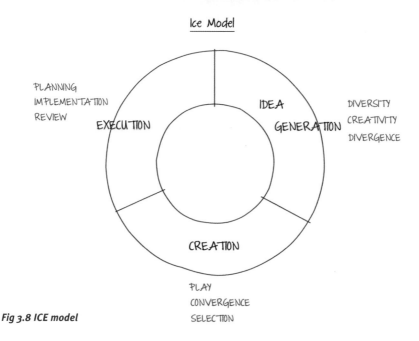

Fig 3.8 ICE model

Sam's frustrated and it's starting to show. Just when the team appear to be closing on a decision, for no apparent reason it seems to open up again with even more ideas and options thrown on the table, no doubt for subsequent clustering and organisation.

Fran can sense that Sam is very tense. In the break he recalls their development day a month earlier when they discovered and shared their learning styles. They'd joked that Sam is a bit isolated in the sense that his approach to learning is very different. He plots them all on the ICE model and it's suddenly clear what is happening.

When the group reconvene, he explains the picture. Sam's learning style is activist, as Sam learns best from having a go or getting involved. The other members of the team are either reflectors, who generally enjoy generating a wide range of ideas, or theorists, who enjoy turning observations into theory. Effectively Sam's on his own on the left-hand side.

Fran comments: 'I think what we've got here is a group of us happy to play in the idea generation phase of the model, because that's our natural style, and Sam, who can't wait to get going with something. Perhaps it also explains why some of our previous plans have struggled to gain momentum once we move to delivery. It's a good job we've got Sam on board; he's in his element then.'

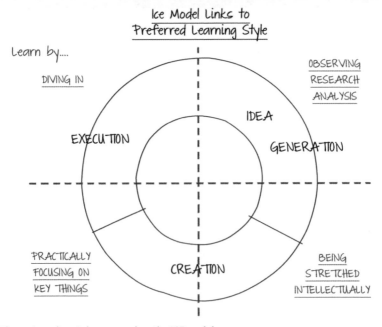

Fig 3.9 Learning styles mapped on the ICE model

The story brings a number of engagement issues we've covered to the fore. Whilst learning style is the aspect where behaviour is different between people in the meeting, it could have been anything. There's no end to the scope for differences between people.

My point is that it takes an appreciation of another's point of view for engagement to happen. Sam's much more comfortable knowing why he's frustrated at this stage in the process. The team are much better as a whole for understanding each other. The open arena has been increased and the team know that with a range of learning styles amongst them they will be more effective throughout all stages of the project.

Fran saw and acknowledged in Sam the value of something different, embracing diversity. Everyone can now see how their own attitude to learning will contribute at certain stages of a project. It also helps them understand how they will be less comfortable at other times in the process. Collaboration builds on everyone's strengths.

The combination of valuing diversity and building on strengths creates successful teams.

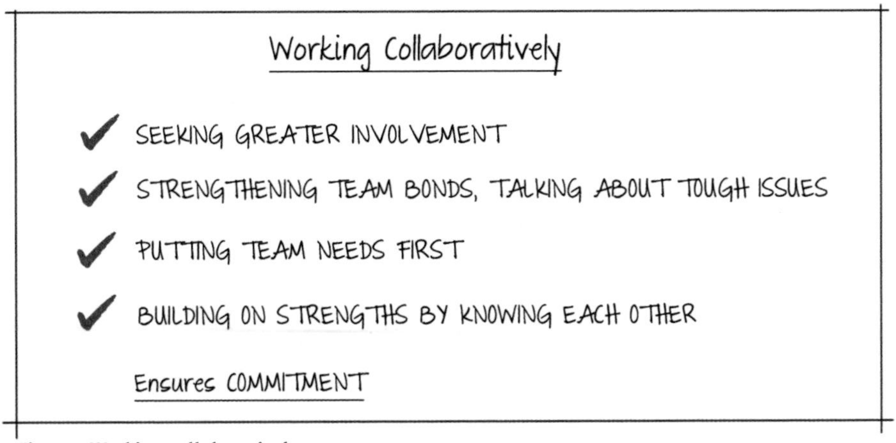

Fig 3.10 Working collaboratively

Leaders build rapport and emotional commitment

This is partly achieved by the way leaders communicate. Open, respectful and honest dialogue creates an atmosphere of trust. Leaders give a great deal of thought to the audience – they make sure people's interventions and discussions are addressed in the right way. They appear to choose intuitively and correctly from a portfolio of alternative approaches. And the style changes or adapts depending on the individual and the situation. They give as much thought to how they are going to be perceived or persuade as to the logic behind the message.

Leaders change their style because consistent leadership, using the same style with everyone on every occasion, doesn't work. That's simply because different people are looking for different things in a leader, and even that may vary depending on the time available or the circumstances. Whilst there may be a science to leadership, in the sense here's the range of behaviours, the art is picking which to use when and with whom.

Being courteous and fair is important. Holding the value that people, all people, are important gives the audience positive energy. Leaders use the rapport they create to influence but always in a non-political manner, whether that's directly or through colleagues. The intent always comes across as genuine.

Smiling builds rapport; it's more a function of how the leader is feeling than what's going on around them. Don't contain that instinct. It says to others: 'It's good to see you' and 'I'm looking forward to our discussion.'

Rapport is also built through how leaders respond to what they see. They always have an eye for people's reactions; they pick up body language and visual cues, which they acknowledge.

Building Rapport/Emotional Commitment

✔ SELECTING THE APPROACH TO SUIT THE PERSON

✔ ADAPTING TO THE AUDIENCE, INTUITIVE

✔ SHOWING HUMAN VALUES, FAIRNESS

✔ SPOTTING VISUAL CLUES AND SUBLIMINAL MESSAGES

Fig 3.11 Building rapport and emotional commitment

Intuition plays a big part in this; leaders know when to cut some slack and when to be insistent. They pick up subliminal messages during conversations and sometimes you will naturally find yourself discussing something you may not have intended to share but now feel very comfortable about. They pick up subtle cues and underlying concerns. Leaders sense, like a radar, where issues lie and probe to surface and then discuss. They have the ability to see through all the static and pick up the things that are important, as Goffee and Jones point out in 'Why

Should Anyone Be Led By You?'[22] They describe 'tough empathy' as leading with a mix of providing direction and engagement, empathising with others without losing sight of the importance of the work they do.[23] They argue it's achieved when leaders communicate authentically. Attending to both the business and the people around you is one of the many balancing acts of leaders.

Leaders are transparent, open and trustworthy

The Kouses and Posner research in 'The Leadership Challenge' identifies honesty as the attribute followers value most.[24] O'Toole and Bennis also say that trustworthiness always tops the list.[25] It's clearly very important. Followers are looking for leaders who are frank and open. The essence of such leaders' message is consistent every time, even with different stakeholders or groups. It's linked to the direction provided in the last chapter. There's a sense of security and confidence that decisions will be made that are consistent with that message, can be explained in the context of it and are not made arbitrarily.

Leaders' conversations are always very frank and honest; they openly express trust in the decisions their teams make. This approach does not change even when faced with a huge range of beliefs, doctrines and philosophies.

Covey uses the concept of an 'emotional bank account' to indicate the level of trust that is invested in a relationship.[26] The elements of engagement that build the account are deposits in Covey's terms, such as showing consideration, listening, showing respect and delivering on your commitments. If you feel your relationship with some people is worse than with others it's worth considering the relative state of the emotional bank accounts. Have you failed to attend to one or made withdrawals? Using a device like this to focus on building trust encourages less frequent use of direct leadership behaviours, the losing behaviours we'll explore in Chapter 6, whilst promoting listening skills.

Whilst their approach and attitude is open, leaders are also open about their feelings. In fact, they'll go beyond being open to explicitly making comments to clarify their feelings with others, leaving others in no doubt. That emotions are visible is perceived very favourably; it's an openness that provides comfort in the relationship. It's the trust that shifts the hidden area into the open arena of the Johari window (Fig 3.3) and takes engagement to a higher level. A huge open or public arena with team mates is openness at its best; blind spots are eliminated through frank but sensitive feedback; and there's the trust to share personal views, feelings and beliefs.

Openness encourages others to confide. People feel they can talk candidly about any situation whether that's the business, personal aspirations or just personal stuff.

> *'Of all my colleagues, she's the one person I immediately turn to if I'm not trusting my own judgement. I know she won't hold back from sharing what she really thinks because she knows me well and I trust her.'*

Sometimes it takes courage for leaders to act in this way; there are feelings for both leaders and others that are associated with complete transparency. They leave themselves open to both constructive feedback and criticism and they engage with brutal honesty. There's courage in sharing thoughts; it's brave to get issues in the open and address them. Leaders believe it's worth having a full debate on contentious topics even though they are aware of the sensitivities.

There are risks to building trust but these can be managed by taking small steps that encourage the other party to respond in kind. Meeting someone halfway is a good example; it doesn't have to be all or nothing. But there is no doubt that any relationship is better for a healthy emotional bank account. Just think about how to use the engagement behaviours to make deposits with people around you.

Collins comments: 'When you conduct autopsies without blame you go a long way to creating a climate where the truth is heard.'[27] There's a perception of no hidden agendas that is created from previous experiences and exchanges with the leader. Trust does not happen spontaneously; it's a fragile but very important feeling that develops over time.

Lencioni identifies a number of behaviours seen once trust is established.[28] Apologies are offered and accepted without hesitation. People admit mistakes and appreciate the talents of others. People are given the benefit of the doubt and take risks in providing feedback. He describes trust as feeling 'comfortable being vulnerable with one another'.

In explaining synergy Covey puts together two elements of engagement: trust and cooperation within collaboration.[29] He argues that only true openness releases a win–win discussion in a relationship or partnership. If there's low trust and low cooperation the outcome will be win–lose dialogue; and if there's medium trust and medium cooperation the conversation will simply be a pleasant compromise.

Transparency has become an imperative from an organisational perspective. Companies need to be ethically as well as commercially sound. Having leaders who role-model the behaviours associated with trust and openness is therefore critical.

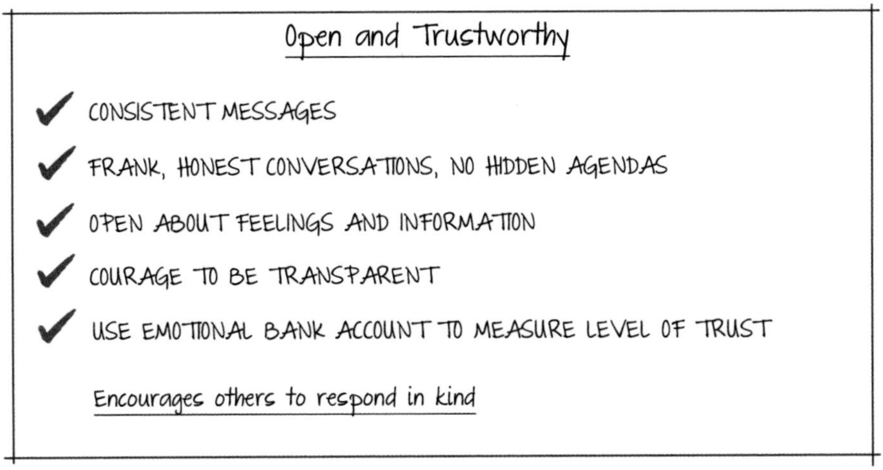

```
┌─────────────────────────────────────────────────────────────┐
│                  Open and Trustworthy                         │
│                                                               │
│  ✔  CONSISTENT MESSAGES                                       │
│                                                               │
│  ✔  FRANK, HONEST CONVERSATIONS, NO HIDDEN AGENDAS            │
│                                                               │
│  ✔  OPEN ABOUT FEELINGS AND INFORMATION                       │
│                                                               │
│  ✔  COURAGE TO BE TRANSPARENT                                 │
│                                                               │
│  ✔  USE EMOTIONAL BANK ACCOUNT TO MEASURE LEVEL OF TRUST     │
│                                                               │
│     Encourages others to respond in kind                      │
│                                                               │
└─────────────────────────────────────────────────────────────┘
```

Fig 3.12 Open and trustworthy

In summary, the behaviours of attentive listening, considering the opinions of and being considerate of other people are applied to build social networks and a collaborative team spirit. Leaders freely share information, and that openness extends to all aspects of leadership. They build rapport and trust. Those are the behaviours associated with engagement.

Engagement embraces two of the Hay Group leadership styles also described by Goleman.[30] First is an affiliative style where the leader is focused on the maintenance and development of strong emotional bonds between them and others around them, a desire for harmony at any cost. Whilst there are clearly downsides if this were the only approach, not least because task is overlooked at the expense of maintaining or creating harmony, such leaders 'are masters at building a sense of belonging'; they are natural relationship builders.

Second is a democratic style that sets aside time for discussion to hear alternative views and create a sense of buy-in through consensus. In this way leaders 'build trust, respect and commitment'. They do this not just in team meetings but also in one-on-one discussions. Goleman describes the behaviours associated with the democratic style as listening and collaboration, working as team members rather than leader and direct report.

Leaders rely heavily on their ability to manage themselves to build emotional commitment and demonstrate transparency but the trust they create will pay dividends.

The overriding theme throughout the range of behaviours associated with engagement is listening. Carnegie, in 'How to Win Friends and Influence People', uses the following description of Sigmund Freud's listening skills attributed to a friend:

It struck me forcibly that I shall never forget him. He had qualities I have never seen in any other man. Never had I seen such concentrated attention. There was none of the piercing 'soul penetrating gaze' business. His eyes were mild and genial. His voice was low and kind. His gestures were few. But the attention he gave me, his appreciation of what I said, even when I said it badly, was extraordinary. You've no idea what it meant to be listened to like that.[31]

Kline tells leaders: 'Listen as if your leadership life depended on it, it does.'[32] The impact of engagement on others is in two areas: creating first a sense that my leader is 'there for me' and second a sense of team spirit. It also helps create a sense of calm in potentially stressful situations.

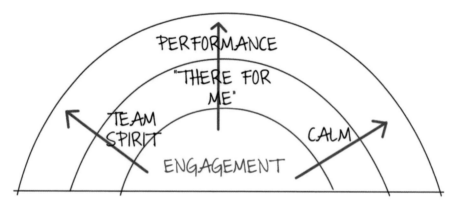

Fig 3.13 Links from engagement through impact on others to performance

So how do you think you do? Have a look at the following diagnostic to assess your strength relative to engagement behaviours.

How Characteristic are the Following for the Leader being Evaluated?

ENGAGEMENT

	NOT AT ALL		SOMEWHAT		VERY	DON'T KNOW
LISTENS ATTENTIVELY	☐	☐	☐	☐	☐	☐
SHOWS CONSIDERATION FOR THE FEELINGS AND NEEDS OF OTHERS	☐	☐	☐	☐	☐	☐
SEEKS AND CONSIDERS THE VIEWS AND OPINIONS OF OTHERS	☐	☐	☐	☐	☐	☐
INVESTS TIME TO CREATE AND MAINTAIN NETWORKS	☐	☐	☐	☐	☐	☐
SHARES RELEVANT INFORMATION, KEEPS PEOPLE UPDATED	☐	☐	☐	☐	☐	☐
WORKS COLLABORATIVELY WITH OTHERS, A TEAM WORKER	☐	☐	☐	☐	☐	☐
BUILDS RAPPORT AND EMOTIONAL COMMITMENT	☐	☐	☐	☐	☐	☐
IS TRANSPARENT, OPEN, TRUSTWORTHY	☐	☐	☐	☐	☐	☐

CHAPTER 4
In The Zone

'He's a fantastic sounding board, always enthusiastic;
he challenges me whilst leaving me the space to get on
with it myself. I feel absolutely empowered in my job.'

Having provided direction and engaged both with individuals and around task, it's time to focus on performance because there is a very important output to leadership. The behaviours we'll discuss in this chapter create a performance oriented culture.

From the research it was clear that there are many different aspects to focusing on performance, that I believe explains why great coaches are held in such high regard. However, labelling the cluster of behaviours as simply coaching misses the many nuances we'll explore. It's the way leaders coach, the behaviours they adopt, which makes the difference.

> A year ago Kim received some poor feedback about the way he 'focuses on performance' with his own team. Since then he's been on a coaching programme and is very enthusiastic about a simple process called GROW, where a goal is established, there's a reality check that it's a genuine issue, options are explored before there's a wrap-up to the session that identifies the next steps.[1]

Grow Model

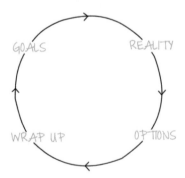

Fig 4.1 GROW model

He loves the simplicity of the process and has religiously followed it in all his one-to-ones with his team for a year. Kim reckons he's probably doubled the amount of coaching he has done. His notes on the GROW model are well thumbed with many further comments he's added himself. Kim has clearly been very busy.

However, in his performance review a year later the feedback from his team is very disappointing. Indeed, it appears that the increased coaching has coincided with a sharp increase in use of the losing behaviours. Kim goes back to the original trainers demanding an explanation.

They ask Kim to talk through his last two coaching sessions and the reason becomes clear. Everything goes smoothly through the g(oal) and r(eality) stages but when it comes to o(ptions) the focus shifts from the person who desires coaching to Kim, partly through his enthusiasm to help. Once the issue is clear Kim jumps in with phrases like: 'Don't worry I've seen that before. Here's what I did;' 'That's clear then, all you need to do is ...' and 'Let me tell you what worked for me.' Attentive listening has gone out of the window as Kim grasps the nettle excited in pursuit of his own solution.

Outstanding coaches work on the other person's agenda and not their own. On occasions, yes, they will make appropriate suggestions but only when they are requested to or sense that input will be appreciated. The activity of coaching can be conducted in any style or behaviour, including those described later as 'losing'.

The distinction between an activity and behaviour is very important. Following the GROW model to conduct the activity of coaching, it's in the option phase where behaviours will be felt. For example, 'Before we explore some alternatives let's remind ourselves where we are going' would be perceived as providing direction. In focusing on performance there is a range of behaviours deployed by leaders to get the most out of people ... but always on others' terms rather than leaders'.

Leaders encourage others to act and take responsibility

The actions and decisions that are encouraged are anchored in the direction provided. Feedback in this regard starts with a statement of how individuals are clear about something or have clarity, and from that comes a desire to get on with it.

'She provides real clarity of direction, leaving individuals the autonomy and support to lead specific work areas themselves.'

Freedom, autonomy and empowerment are words used to describe the positive feelings associated with this behaviour. Leaders empower with confidence and trust. There's a release in providing complete licence to act within very broad parameters, an unusual and heady mix of clarity with freedom. Empowerment leaves people with the perception that it's completely acceptable to challenge the way things are done and that they are totally accountable for the change themselves.

Leaders have the uncanny knack of giving people sufficient responsibility to feel stretched. They use the people skills from the engagement behaviours to gauge this just right. It's as much as they desire or can handle. They will check to ensure everything is aligned with priorities or the vision but without giving the feeling they doubt anyone's ability.

Alongside confidence and trust, leaders empower with real enthusiasm. There is something highly energising about a combination of challenging debate and leaving people the space to manage their part of the organisation themselves.

When this faith is seen not to waver, even through difficult times, it is unique and makes that organisation a special place to work.

It's the last night of a series of roadshows, a chance to meet all the people in the organisation, share the corporate vision, take questions and listen to concerns. As with every other evening, Sam is pinned in a corner taking feedback on the quality of the staff uniform. Whether it's the biggest issue facing the organisation is debatable but what is beyond dispute is that this is a hot topic and certainly the most frequently raised. Tonight, colleague encouragement has led to one of the more vociferous attacks.

The following morning Sam calls the 'ring leader' who rather sheepishly starts to apologise for his outburst. Sam tells him not to worry and that his depth of feeling has been shared by many over the last two weeks. He asks whether he will take responsibility for selecting a new uniform. Sam will agree the budget with him and offer whatever resource is required to research opinion, draw up a specification, tender, select a supplier and launch the new uniform.

Three months later, the proposal is presented to Sam. The new uniform is favourably received and all queries regarding the project are dealt with by the team themselves. The new uniform has lasted longer than anything previously used and the talk at the following year's roadshow is how successful the staff's own initiative has been.

Sam reflects on how much of his time could have been spent on this but still not getting that kind of result. Why do things yourself when others are far more capable? Empowerment frees up a leader's time whilst motivating others through the responsibility given.

It's worth considering how many of the tasks you currently undertake as a leader could be done better by one of your team and with more enthusiasm.

Empowerment is the only choice when you have outstanding direct reports with both the ability and motivation to perform. In geographically diverse organisations or where service is delivered remotely, providing autonomy is key. As a leader you can't rely on red tape and rules relayed from the centre. Indeed, if central bureaucracy is required to get things done then the leaders themselves become the constraint or bottleneck to timely decision making.

People genuinely value empowerment but where it is done without context or boundaries it is perceived as desertion rather than delegation. Without the clarity of clear direction and the availability of a leader's support as a sounding board, or whatever guise, it's viewed as a 'losing behaviour', as abdication.

Pink identifies autonomy, 'the desire to direct our own lives', as critical to motivation.[2] People want autonomy over task (what they do), time (when to do it), team (who they do it with) and technique (how they do it). It's a good way of considering whether you have exhausted all the dimensions empowerment offers. Why not use it as a checklist?

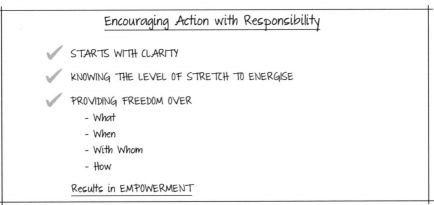

Fig 4.2 Encouraging action with responsibility

Leaders encourage new ideas and ways of looking at things
Empowerment, in itself, encourages fresh thinking. Leaders role-model these behaviours themselves, they enjoy challenging debates that throw up new ideas,

and their openness extends to ideas and concepts that are personally threatening.

'He thrives on change, he invites it and challenge is his tactic.'

Challenging the status quo comes naturally. You'll hear leaders say: 'Is this the only option?' or 'What about taking a different approach?'

There are so many ways to kill new ideas at source – 'Been there, done that;' 'It won't work here;' and so on – but leaders do the opposite. They give ideas the chance to flourish before jointly concluding whether there are better options. They are not anchored to past dictums or routines that, although safe, do not position the organisation for a future in which it distances itself from its competitors.

Leaders encourage people to try something new, and take a balanced risk to find a better way.

'Faced with an exceptional situation he asks us: what exceptional action will we take to meet this threat or grab this opportunity?'

If the leader feels people are blinded by routine he'll give them a polite nudge. They ask incisive questions that remove limiting assumptions and encourage freedom to think beyond old boundaries. They create a culture where creativity is valued, one of continuous questioning.

Not everyone is interested in and enthusiastic about new ideas. Strebel identifies a number of ways people respond to change, with two types of people relevant here.[3] The first he describes as traditionalists, who feel secure, for whatever reason, in the maintenance of the status quo. A second group he describes as resistors, who see their power threatened by potential change. It's therefore naive to assume everyone is open to change and new ideas. The engagement behaviours we discussed in the last chapter give leaders a feel for the type of reluctance they are likely to encounter so they can prepare accordingly.

A healthy attitude to the value diversity brings will help. We tend to surround ourselves with people who are like us, 'like minded souls', but when we can finish our colleagues' sentences for them what are the chances of exploring a bold new position? Some, as Strebel suggests, have a vested interest in the status quo. It's a tough nut for a leader to crack if they, themselves, are part of the problem and don't even realise it.

Diversity is about our ability to immerse ourselves in the culture around us, getting in touch with reality. Boxes seem natural; we put words in them and there's a warmth that comes from being safely inside. Learning organisations encourage people to go beyond the confines, to go 'out of the box'. The box analogy is one way to consider the constraints of maintaining the status quo. Why be constrained by the possibilities inside such a small structure?

Fig 4.3 Encouraging new ideas

Leaders put energy, time and focus into personal coaching

The affiliative motive is the need to satisfy a desire to be liked by others and, on the face of it, coaching offers an opportunity to satisfy that need.[4] Coaching should not, however, be considered a chance to become more popular. The priority is to achieve performance through others. Looking at the affiliative motive from another perspective, if you really wish to be liked and respected, I recommend that you try focusing on helping others succeed, which will certainly please them.

Responsibility for improving performance does not rest with the leader. However, it is the leader's responsibility to offer coaching, feedback and the opportunity to develop. That's their part of the contract.

Outstanding coaches create a special feeling in others of being the centre of attention, with the coach focused 100 per cent on them. Others know that the leader, as a coach, has business priorities but within the coaching conversation such priorities don't arise. The attention is exclusively on the individual's needs or concerns and the leader appears to be able to see and feel everything from their point of view without distraction. Only then can leaders leverage the very best out of their people, when it is on their terms.

Leaders start with the view that people have different characteristics – what the leader may perceive as illogical is perfectly normal to others. Our outlook on life stems from our early childhood and as a result, when faced with similar circumstances, our paradigm of life prompts a set of responses and behaviours that is personal to us.

Leaders value diversity: through listening and observing they understand diversity from each individual's point of view. They use insightful questioning to develop a real understanding of the issues facing people. They then help people work out for themselves the best way forward whilst still offering constructive challenge and probing to understand why it's the best solution ... and of course they check alignment with priorities.

There's a sense that nothing is too much trouble if it will assist with personal development. In casual conversation with leaders it's usual for an aspect of development to emerge, simply because it's so important to leaders. It may be filling a vacancy, a discussion about someone recently promoted or some ideas on a proposed training programme. They are interested in personal development plans, willingly provide feedback and are relentlessly on the search for opportunities to stretch individuals and enable them to play to their strengths.

After intense discussion about development, leaders then delegate well and take a back seat, available as a sounding board if required. For leaders the performance review is a great way to demonstrate this focus. The quality of their feedback, selecting others to provide feedback, sensitively sharing feedback and working with others to identify the things that will make the biggest difference to their leadership; these are what fill people with confidence about their own abilities. They create a reassuring environment and bring serenity to the resolution of issues.

'He is part coach, parent, confessor and teacher. He does all these things well because he is genuinely interested in the success of his team.'

Putting Energy into Personal Coaching

✓ PROVIDING ENCOURAGEMENT BUT NOT TAKING RESPONSIBILITY FOR THE PERFORMANCE OF OTHERS

✓ LEAVING OTHERS FEELING LIKE THERE WAS COMPLETE FOCUS ON THEM

✓ HELPING PEOPLE WORK THINGS OUT FOR THEMSELVES

✓ ALWAYS HAVING TIME FOR PERSONAL DEVELOPMENT

✓ DELEGATING WITH CONFIDENCE

Turns TALENT into PERFORMANCE

Fig 4.4 Putting energy into personal coaching

Leaders build a reputation, a track record for developing others; it's another thing that attracts people to their teams. But they don't confine their impact to just their own teams; they get involved in development issues more broadly, whether that's helping with assessment, induction, and coaching or providing insightful feedback from interactions with people.

Buckingham and Coffman describe great managers as those who turn talent into performance: 'They are the catalysts that speed up the reaction between each person's talents and the company's goals.'[5] You can see the hook back to the importance of a vision providing context and the familiar Buckingham theme of identifying and playing to people's strengths.

Leaders remove barriers, creating space and opportunity to develop

They help overcome constraints and make high level interventions where it is appropriate. Leaders will do anything to remove a barrier that inhibits performance. Our working lives are an endless list of things to do but leaders don't neglect the need to create time for people to generate ideas and solve problems; they simply see it as a way to reduce that list rather than an additional task. It's a completely different mindset to that which we'll see with losing behaviours, where leaders feel responsible for working through the list themselves.

Leaders are always alert to projects or roles to develop people, anxious to provide every opportunity to grow and develop in a coaching and nurturing environment. When a secondment opportunity arises in a meeting you can imagine some leaders saying, 'I'll inform the head of HR about that.' Occasionally someone will say, 'I know just the person for that role; it's exactly what they have been looking for.' It's simply front of mind for leaders. They recall the detail of the development conversation instantly because it's important to them; they see it as part of their job to seek out development opportunities that are specific to individuals.

Leaders offer support in development, whether that's a discussion about performance, a conversation about the impact on others, some informal feedback, encouragement to take risks or the budget to take action. They will volunteer to help on training programmes to demonstrate visibly their belief in and commitment to development.

Leaders are comfortable learning from mistakes; they see this as part of development. They will create a non-critical setting to share experience, help draw conclusions and move on. They will avoid getting involved too early, leaving others to resolve their issues or problems in their own way. They get the right balance between standing back whilst always being available as a sounding board.

When others are learning by doing, which is a big part of leadership development, the leader as a coach plays a crucial role providing time to review and discuss which behaviours are working but need to be reinforced, and which are less effective and require a different approach. Creating time to reflect, explore and offer a sounding board is essential. Whilst the tenets of leadership are clear, applying that logic requires practice and constant refinement. Leaders help others through this process.

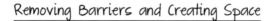

Removing Barriers and Creating Space

✓ SEEING TIME SPENT WITH OTHERS AS AN INVESTMENT

✓ ACTIVELY SEEKING STRETCH TASKS FOR OTHERS TO DEVELOP

✓ COMFORTABLE LEARNING FROM MISTAKES

✓ ENCOURAGING TIME FOR REFLECTION

OVERCOMES CONSTRAINTS and provides a SOUNDING BOARD

Fig 4.5 Removing barriers and creating space

Leaders accurately assess the strengths and weaknesses of others

They get to know people thoroughly using the behaviours we discussed in engagement. Leaders read people accurately; they understand what makes them tick through a combination of close observation and active listening. They are aware not just of relative strengths and weaknesses but also of personal and career aspirations.

Leaders play to the strengths of the individuals in their team. They encourage people to take responsibility in areas where they are strong; as a result people get increased confidence from that responsibility and feel valued. They will also look for opportunities to promote those strengths. They are not blind to the weaknesses; they simply see playing to strengths as having greater impact.

Buckingham and Coffman argue that 'People don't change that much. Don't waste time trying to put in what was left out. Try to draw out what was left in. That is hard enough.'[6] Everyone has talents – discover and help people strengthen them.

It's one thing to identify strengths and weaknesses and another to share that knowledge. To test this, rank your own team into upper and lower quartile and average performance, then read through the feedback you shared in their last performance review. Do the comments in the reviews reinforce your ranking? I'd expect to see a stark difference especially in the line manager's (your) summary. If there isn't, chances are you are not getting your message across and as a manager you are likely to be seen as someone who can't differentiate between outstanding, average and poor performance.

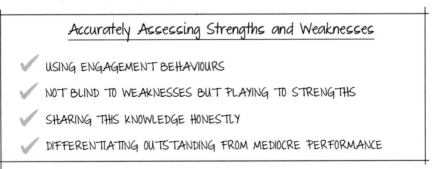

Fig 4.6 Accurately assessing strengths and weaknesses

Leaders provide constructive, impactful feedback

Even if feedback is balanced, equally positive and negative, people tend to recall the negative. Roberts, Spreitzer, Dutton, Quinn, Heaphy and Barker explain that 'when asked to recall important emotional events, people remembered four negative memories for every positive one'.[7] That's a balance the leader as coach must redress and explains why few look forward to performance reviews and appraisals. They go on to say: 'It's a paradox of human psychology that while people remember criticism, they respond to praise. The former makes them defensive while the latter produces the confidence and desire to perform better.'

We tend to fret over sharing feedback that may be unfavourably received, but first let's remind ourselves of the power of positive feedback and appreciation. Carnegie describes the giving of honest and sincere feedback as a fundamental technique in handling people.[8] 'People will cherish your words and treasure them and repeat them over for a lifetime, repeat them years after you have forgotten them.'

LaFasto and Larson maintain that giving and receiving feedback ensures a relationship is self-correcting.[9]

Leaders give feedback in a way that is both thoughtful and thought provoking. They are particularly sensitive when giving feedback where the individual is blind to the behaviour or impact it is having. Revisiting the Johari window, they have no qualms embracing the feelings associated with giving and receiving feedback because the value of a bigger public arena is far bigger than avoiding the discussion.[10]

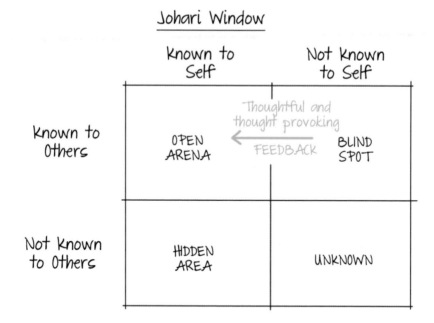

Fig 4.7 Johari window

'She gives feedback directly, precisely and always with respect.'

People sometimes describe open feedback as being brutal, in the sense that it's a shock if they were blind to it, but a recurring theme is that afterwards they are grateful. They appreciate the thought and consideration the leader put into sharing 'the revelation'.

Leaders provide feedback that has an impact; it prompts a reaction. People observe the link between the receipt of feedback and its impact on performance. It's the clarity of the feedback that encourages a response: this is what I saw or felt followed by the impact it has on me, others, the team, the project. With such clarity, insight and delivered sensitively, it's difficult not to feel moved to do something differently. For example, contrast 'I saw you interrupt Harry' with 'I saw you interrupt Harry and he never spoke after that; he just switched off so we'll never know what his view was'.

In providing feedback, leaders look for the sequence we've described as denial through anger to acceptance. They see an emotional release as people go through this process as a positive indication of change. Where possible they focus on the positive aspect of being aware of the impact of behaviour: 'Now you understand this, can you imagine how others will view a change in style from you?'

Two more quotes serve as a timely reminder to us to focus as much on praise and the behaviours that are working as on the things that are not. The first is from psychologist Lair: 'Praise is like sunlight to the warm human spirit; we cannot flower and grow without it. And yet, while most of us are only too ready to apply to others the cold wind of criticism, we are somehow reluctant to give our fellow the warm sunshine of praise.'[11] And the second is from Carnegie: 'History is replete with striking illustrations of the sheer witchery of praise.'[12] People need constantly reminding of the tools in their leadership toolkit they already have – when some are having a positive impact, they need to be encouraged to use and develop those strengths still further.

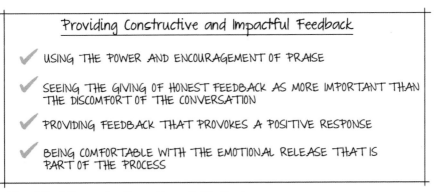

Fig 4.8 Providing constructive and impactful feedback

Leaders focus on delivery with a relentless pursuit of goals

Collins, in 'Good to Great', describes a culture of discipline: 'Throughout our research we were struck by the continual use of words like disciplined, rigorous, dogged, determined, diligent, precise, focus, fastidious, systematic, methodical, workmanlike, demanding, consistent, focused, accountable and responsible' [13]. They are used to describe good to great companies. He suggests that it's as much about avoiding what you shouldn't be doing as focusing on your priorities, stop lists being as important as 'to do' lists.

Leaders know that failure to hit targets or make progress can lead to anxiety and indecisiveness, reducing commitment and confidence. Hence, having the discipline to demonstrate results are being delivered is very important.

Leaders role-model these behaviours themselves. They respond quickly and decisively to threats and opportunities. After accepting responsibility they push constantly for improvements every day. Leaders are incredibly tenacious: meeting deadlines and achieving targets are matters of principle.

'When he commits to something you can take it to the bank.'

Leaders appear to have an abundance of energy that instils urgency. They pursue answers and improvements, irrespective of how long it will take or what sacrifices they'll need to make to achieve their ends. And through motivation they encourage others to display the same behaviours; they show excitement at high standards or with people who go 'the extra mile'. There's a constant enthusiasm with a clear purpose to every conversation with leaders.

People are unlikely to be relentless in pursuit of goals unless such goals are linked to something that is relevant, something they feel a commitment to. As a consequence it's confusing if a leader does not encourage measurement of the things that make the biggest difference, those that are linked to the direction provided.

Measurement is critical when focusing on delivery, as without it you can't quantify progress. Sports are the best examples of this, where there are tables and scores for everything. Measurement provides a degree of independence and empowerment in the sense that the leader's presence is no longer necessary to keep score. Agreeing the key measures with a boss releases people from the vagaries of a leader's subsequent subjective measure of an individual's performance in a review. The assessment becomes totally within the individual's own control.

As being able to keep the score objectively is the best way to measure progress, there's a diagnostic to complement this book. You can assess your relative strength in winning (and losing) behaviours, which in my experience encourages development.

In 'Drive', Pink argues that people are motivated by mastery: 'Mastery begins with "flow", optimal experiences where the challenges we face are exquisitely matched to our abilities.'[14] Flow is described in research conducted by Hay Insight as '[e]ngag[ing] employees and boost[ing] performance'. The term 'flow' is attributed to psychologist Mihalyi Csikzentmahalyi.[15] 'People in flow are exhilarated and are remarkably unstressed even when doing challenging work. They lose themselves in a task they love and feel "out of time".' Their brains work efficiently and precisely. Flow occurs most often when tasks are tightly aligned with the person's goals; hence, someone in flow is completely immersed in a task.

Pink goes on to describe mastery as a mindset where there's a belief in sustainable improvement that begs the conclusion that people never get to complete mastery with all the emotions it entails.[16] It also comes at the cost of relentless practice and determination. Pink describes mastery not as something a leader 'does' to their team but as a natural motivation inspired within other people. For the leader as coach the challenge is working with the emotions associated with mastery: relentlessly questing for a desired goal that'll never be achieved whilst managing the frustration of knowing it will always be tantalisingly out of reach.

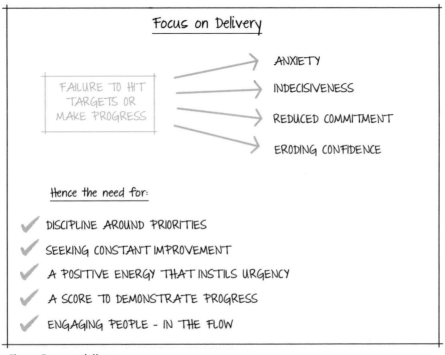

Fig 4.9 Focus on delivery

Leaders make appropriate recommendations
Unlike the tell style we'll explore in losing behaviours, there are times when unprompted contributions are gratefully received. These contributions are not necessarily restricted to the leader's field; he will have opinions on problems and opportunities in other areas.

These recommendations are received in the spirit of being both timely and helpful.

'His input is always useful and often thought provoking, driving a more considered decision from teams that he is involved with.'

Some people refer to these recommendations as 'golden tips' – information only the leader could pass on and for which they are grateful.

Leaders set clear expectations and high standards

Buckingham emphasises the importance of this: 'Define clear expectations. Confusion retards everything, how can you distinguish a short cut from a distraction if you don't know what the goal is?'[17]

Leaders paint a clear picture not only of the future but also of the goals and standards that will take the organisation there. When records are broken they are swift to recognise and celebrate but just as swift to move on to the next record. Beating targets is something that is apparent in every conversation. Leaders are animated by high standards; they share and sell them with huge conviction. They cultivate a culture of records on every front, and love telling stories about them.

There is a positive energy in the group when standards are perceived as stretching, as leaders know the power of a stretch target that people perceive as possible to achieve.

'She does not accept a point of diminishing returns; we get the sense that records are there to be broken forever.'

The concept of stretch comes from an open discussion on what can be achieved when barriers are removed and an individual has complete support. Without that conversation there is simply apprehension about targets.

A simple game brings home to Alex how complex setting goals can be. They are asked to enter a room one at a time, where there is a peg and tape marked out in varying multiples of 1 ft intervals from the peg. They are given three rings and asked to choose a distance and say how many rings they will get on the peg. He tries to get more information but nothing is forthcoming. Alex goes for 1 ft and lands all three rings on the peg. Despite some anxiety and hand-shaking, he achieves his target.

In the second round they are all in the room together, with the results from the first round on the board. Alex is to go first again, but this time with everyone milling around. He glances at the results, wondering whether they were asked the same question the first time, because someone went for two rings from 16 ft. Why would they have done that? Alex decides to be a bit more adventurous and goes for three rings from 2 ft. He succeeds but there's little interest from the audience.

When ring-tossers are either too close or too far away others looking on are generally uninterested. Engagement comes when the target is between 8 and 12 ft from the peg. Energy levels are high and there's tension in the room. In a third round they're asked to pay to play to win a reward commensurate with distance and the number of rings on the peg.

The conclusion from the exercise is that behaviour is a function of two things: the individual (everyone sets different goals given the same question); and the situation (the goal chosen varies depending on whether you are alone, in a group or when rewards are offered as incentive).

Alex took away much more. He thought about the budget target agreed with Group: he was comfortable with it but he started pondering where the others stood and how energised they were by the target. He thought of other parts of the business where they were all focused on the same target, where presumably they also had different attitudes to risk and targets? There appeared to be many dimensions to goal setting, including fear of failure, anticipation of success, the reward dimension, peer pressure and personal attitude to risk. Yet throughout the business there were often common targets set for all, in the interest of fairness.

Alex concluded, firstly, that whilst standards are important, it's not the leader's standards that energise; a leader needs to find that zone of creative tension between anxiety about failure and the sweet sense of success for each of his team. Secondly, where there can only be one target a leader needs to find other ways to motivate, recognition, for example.

At his next one-to-one with Sam he suggests: 'I know we need to agree a target with Group for customer service but, given whatever resource you need, what do you believe we can achieve?' Sam gives Alex a sceptical look. 'Are you thinking of changing the bonus target?' 'Absolutely not,' replies Alex, 'I'm just interested in your view.' That's the start of many stimulating conversations on the topic, because Sam is in the zone.

This is one of the most researched simulations to understand goal setting behaviour.[18] It never fails to capture the imagination of those involved, as how can people react so differently to the same brief? The relevance to us is: whose agenda, standards and values are you coaching against?

People with a high achievement drive will thrive on stretch targets, provided they are accomplished. Given support and encouragement they will, not surprisingly, get a real buzz from achieving goals. The leader's task is to identify the strength of that motive in others and, through discussion, be clear on the extent of their zone of creative tension. Failure impacts the confidence of such individuals in particular.

Lencioni describes the 'avoidance of accountability' as one of the 'Five Dysfunctions of a Team'.[19] He puts another perspective on standards by suggesting that the best way to maintain high standards is peer pressure, which is created through people holding each other accountable. In this way difficult conversations take place with frank but constructive feedback. Issues are surfaced, poor performance raised and as a result there's respect between peers. It supports, but does not eliminate the leader's responsibility to deliver high standards and it certainly builds team commitment.

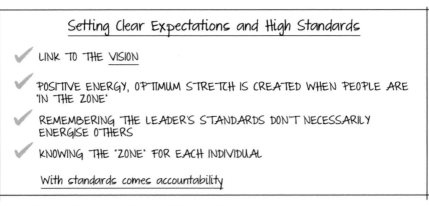

Setting Clear Expectations and High Standards

✓ LINK TO THE VISION

✓ POSITIVE ENERGY, OPTIMUM STRETCH IS CREATED WHEN PEOPLE ARE 'IN THE ZONE'

✓ REMEMBERING THE LEADER'S STANDARDS DON'T NECESSARILY ENERGISE OTHERS

✓ KNOWING THE 'ZONE' FOR EACH INDIVIDUAL

With standards comes accountability

Fig 4.10 Setting clear expectations and high standards

Leaders reward performance

Leaders understand the art of motivation through both words and gifts that are highly appreciated. Specifically, anything that contributes to progress towards the chosen direction is recognised. Whether that recognition is in private or public, the expression of genuine gratitude that accompanies it is impactful.

Leaders do this consistently; they never fail to recognise and acknowledge high performance in anyone. They take personal satisfaction in the success of others, regularly recognising achievement beyond their own area with as much enthusiasm as they would their own team.

Leaders use rewards to motivate and encourage through picturing positive expectations such as: 'Imagine how it will feel when …' Recognition is particularly welcomed when progress is tough or when people are feeling uncertain about themselves or the project. It's that bit of encouragement to push onwards, to believe it's all worth it. It gives people a boost.

Leaders can also spot outstanding performance and openly show it. Linked to the behaviours associated with high standards, leaders work on an assumption that the average constrains performance. They look at who is 'best in class' and hold them up as the exemplar.

> Two of Chris's team have been heavily involved in the implementation of an IT system for the past year. Last week they went live and it is widely regarded as successful throughout the organisation.
>
> As his finance team meeting closes Chris presents a bottle of champagne to all six members of his team and thanks everyone for their contribution to a smooth go-live. The gift is appreciated but not the recognition. As they leave the room one is heard to mutter, 'I just don't understand why we've all got a bottle. Why didn't Chris give three bottles to the two who did all the work?'

In rewarding everyone, perhaps through Chris's desire to please all his team (the affiliative motive described earlier), he's belittling the effort put in by those who did all the work and it's not lost on those who didn't. Far from pleasing everyone, Chris pleased nobody.

People respect a leader who acknowledges outstanding performance. They look for 'Well done, team, but in particular I'd like to thank … because …' If the 'because' is linked to the vision in providing direction, all the better. People who aren't recognised like to know that when they do deserve it they will be singled out for praise. It's the anticipation of praise rightly earned and deserved.

Recognising superior performance simply reinforces a culture of high standards.

You can't over praise. Recognition is encouragement to repeat the behaviour. Choosing not to, simply to avoid complacency, will have the opposite effect. Whatever the skill someone is trying to develop, becoming world class is the result of a winning behaviour becoming completely natural through practice and refinement, a combination of constant recognition and feedback.

A recurring theme in focus on performance is that everyone is different, so targeting rewards that appeal to each individual is key, whether that's publicly or in private, through words, promotion, gift or bonus.

Kouses and Posner, in 'Encouraging the Heart', identify the key aspects of this winning behaviour.[20] Leaders link reward to what's important to the organisation; they're on the look-out for examples and they expect they'll find them. They personalise rewards but do it publically to 'celebrate together' by 'telling a story' and 'setting an example'. They role-model the behaviours associated with reward.

```
┌─────────────────────────────────────────────────────────────┐
│                  Rewarding Performance                        │
│                                                               │
│  ✓  MOTIVATING THROUGH WORDS AND GIFTS - CONSISTENTLY AND     │
│     EVERYWHERE                                                │
│                                                               │
│  ✓  CLEARLY RECOGNISING 'BEST IN CLASS'                       │
│                                                               │
│  ✓  SPOTTING SUPERIOR PERFORMANCES TO REINFORCE THE IMPORTANCE│
│     OF HIGH STANDARDS                                         │
│                                                               │
│     Recognition is the encouragement to repeat behaviour      │
│                                                               │
└─────────────────────────────────────────────────────────────┘
```

Fig 4.11 Rewarding performance

Leaders advocate the sharing of best practice

They take every opportunity to point out that someone else must have solved the same problem before and discuss where to search for that solution. The leader's underlying belief is that sharing best practice is far better and quicker than 'reinventing the wheel'. They are keen to set up scorecards to measure people and departments that do the same thing as a way to assess who does it best so everyone can learn.

'Always points out that we can learn so much from each other.'

If there are teams in your organisation doing the same thing measured in the same way, it's a rich source of learning and great potential for constant improvement. The curiosity we saw in providing direction and the networking in engagement combine here to produce leaders who live rather than just share best practice. They import as well as export and there's a relentless quest to better what they have learnt or adapt it to their own circumstances.

Sometimes ego gets in the way of living best practice. People either protect what they know or want the recognition that's attached to exporting it: 'I was first.' Leaders recognise the value of both importing and exporting best practice. When an issue is raised in conversation they will say: 'Have you talked to?' or 'Who else do you think has solved this problem?' They will use their network developed in engagement to point people in the right direction.

Advocate the Sharing of Best Practice

✓ SHOWING A BELIEF THAT ITS QUICKER AND BETTER THAN 'REINVENTING THE WHEEL'

✓ SETTING UP SCORECARDS TO LEARN

✓ IMPORTING AS WELL AS EXPORTING IDEAS

✓ USING NETWORKS

Fig 4.12 Advocate the sharing of best practice

Leaders tackle poor performance

People resent the presence of underperformers in their team and look to their leader to do something about it.

Leaders act as soon as they observe poor performance or behaviour; they simply don't like to leave people labouring through lack of feedback. They tackle poor performance whilst demonstrating their support and desire to help.

'She will not hesitate to let you know when expectations are not being met.'

They do this both within their own teams and beyond, always supported by constructive feedback. Leaders use polite and measured tones whilst still making it perfectly clear that mediocrity will not be tolerated. So whilst nothing goes unsaid it is conveyed in such a way that the individual still feels valued and encouraged to change.

Leaders do not tackle poor performance publicly. That would certainly lack sensitivity, so sometimes there can be a feeling that issues are not being addressed. However, over time, leaders build a reputation for spotting poor performance or the impact of poor behaviour and resolve it, one way or another.

Lencioni describes the danger of choosing popularity over accountability.[21] Leaders who are reluctant to provide negative feedback run the risk of failing to hold people accountable for their behaviour and results, and consequently others perceive this as unfair. Don't let a desire to be liked get in the way of holding others accountable. No one respects such leadership, including the person who could benefit from the feedback.

Tackling poor performance can feel uncomfortable. But let's remind ourselves of the responsibilities here. The individual is ultimately responsible for performance, but if their leader is aware of instances where that person's impact could be greater it is the leader's duty to share that knowledge.

Cottrell and Layton offer a checklist in 'The Manager's Coaching Handbook'.[22] They argue that a leader needs to be satisfied that eight climate check questions are addressed before employees can be held accountable for their performance. Has the leader provided clear and reasonable expectations, skills training if appropriate, and an explanation of why doing the job well is important, made them accountable (including explaining the consequences of continued poor performance), described the rewards, genuinely empowered and ensured the removal of barriers to success? If the leader provides these and has evidence that they have done so, they can be confident that all that is hindering performance is the individual themselves.

The climate checklist mirrors the aspects of focus on performance we've discovered in this chapter. Where it's helpful is giving leaders confidence that they have done their utmost to tackle poor performance and that what happens next is largely out of their hands. The consequences have been made clear and are understood.

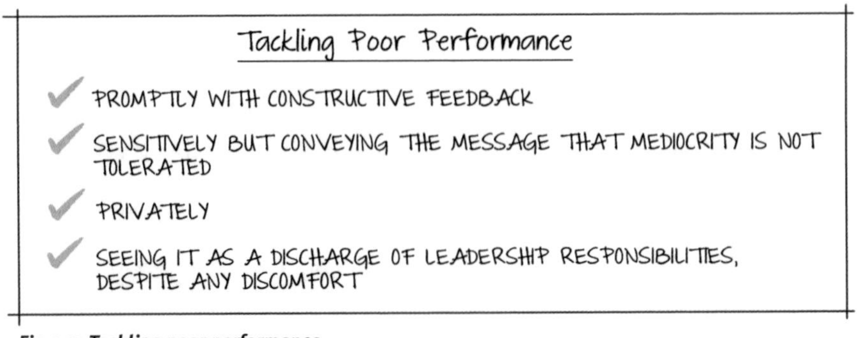

Tackling Poor Performance

✓ PROMPTLY WITH CONSTRUCTIVE FEEDBACK

✓ SENSITIVELY BUT CONVEYING THE MESSAGE THAT MEDIOCRITY IS NOT TOLERATED

✓ PRIVATELY

✓ SEEING IT AS A DISCHARGE OF LEADERSHIP RESPONSIBILITIES, DESPITE ANY DISCOMFORT

Fig 4.13 Tackling poor performance

Leaders provide timely and constructive challenge

Creative challenge is very different from critical challenge, which is much more judgemental.

Leaders challenge others to explore more options and check nothing has been overlooked by insightful questioning. Skilful questions ensure further thought and discussion, rather than simply adding the leader's perspective and seeking quick closure. Empowered high performance leadership is maintained with tactful challenge, around alignment with strategy, for example.

*'She challenges in a positive way, which fosters a
discussion culture and enhances the team as a result.'*

They achieve this whilst building engagement rather than compromising it. It's welcomed especially when someone is about to embark on a new project. The challenge is seen positively as a sounding board before they dive into the initiative. With the spirit of challenge comes a motivational experience and greater confidence. Leaders seem to know the time and place when challenges will be productive and helpful.

Leaders challenge the status quo and assumptions, often taking completely different stakeholder perspectives to ensure all bases are covered.

Leaders see the value of personal development

'Developing leadership capability is his raison d'être.
This is something he does with real passion.'

Leaders take a very broad view of personal development. They ensure there's a level playing field for everyone. Starting with recruitment, they are meticulous on selection, preferring to start the process again where the standard required is not met. They will also consult widely throughout the recruitment process to help shape their view. They will favour neither internal nor external candidates, simply focusing on the behaviours to perform exceptionally in the role.

They ensure training and coaching are available to support career development, and will always take an interest in progress. The enthusiasm leaders show for this puts a marker down for the value it will bring. They are proactive in assessing skills gaps organisationally. Leaders put as much effort into retaining their high performance people as they do into retaining key customers.

Leaders plan for succession. It's sufficient just to identify successors and specifically delegate greater responsibility to them; they feel no need to make it more explicit. Leaders see succession, internal movements and secondments as positive opportunities rather than tasks to be done on a checklist or even inconveniences.

*'The leap of faith he made investing in leadership is
paying dividends today and into the future.'*

Valuing personal development is seeking a fit between the person's strength and the role. Leaders don't leave people struggling in a role that does not suit them even if that means moving to a new role outside the organisation.

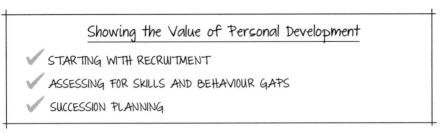

Fig 4.14 Showing the value of personal development

The contrast between focusing on the leader's agenda as opposed to others' agendas is summarised by Goleman, Boyatzis and McKee when describing the Hay Group pacesetting and coaching styles respectively.[23]

The pacesetting style originates in the leader's belief that his standards are the highest and need to be applied. It results in eagerness to get things done to the leader's standard that comes across as demanding and overbearing. They can become so focused on excellence that they appear not to care about people. We'll explore this style in more detail when we consider losing behaviours.

The coaching style focuses on identifying the individual's unique strengths. It involves knowing them on a deep rather than superficial level, and there's an underlying belief in the potential to improve and an expectation that they will deliver that comes from the depth to the relationship. There's an emotional commitment that comes from the empathy shown. 'It may not scream bottom line

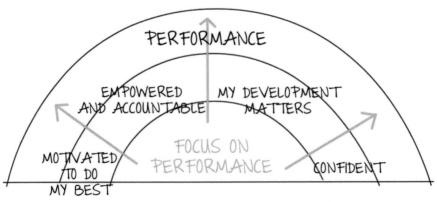

Fig 4.15 Links from focus on performance through impact on others to performance

results but, in a surprisingly indirect way, does deliver them.'

The impact of a focus on performance on others is that they feel inspired and motivated to give their best; they feel empowered and accountable. There's also a feeling that the leader is contributing to individuals' personal development, for which there is gratitude. People have greater confidence in their ability.

We've looked at the many dimensions to focusing on performance. I was personally surprised how many facets there are compared with the other winning behaviours. That's a big challenge for the leader as coach to get results from his people. How do you fare on this range of behaviours? Assess yourself on the diagnostic overleaf.

THE WINNING BEHAVIOURS

<u>How Characteristic are the Following
for the Leader being Evaluated?</u>

FOCUS ON PERFORMANCE

	NOT AT ALL		SOMEWHAT		VERY	DON'T KNOW
ENCOURAGES OTHERS TO ACT AND TAKE RESPONSIBILITY	☐	☐	☐	☐	☐	☐
ENCOURAGES NEW IDEAS AND WAYS OF LOOKING AT THINGS	☐	☐	☐	☐	☐	☐
PUTS ENERGY, TIME AND FOCUS INTO PERSONAL COACHING	☐	☐	☐	☐	☐	☐
REMOVES BARRIERS, CREATES SPACE AND OPPORTUNITY TO DEVELOP	☐	☐	☐	☐	☐	☐
ACCURATELY ASSESSES STRENGTHS AND WEAKNESSES OF OTHERS	☐	☐	☐	☐	☐	☐
PROVIDES CONSTRUCTIVE IMPACTFUL FEEDBACK	☐	☐	☐	☐	☐	☐
FOCUSED ON DELIVERY AND THE RELENTLESS PURSUIT OF GOALS	☐	☐	☐	☐	☐	☐
MAKES APPROPRIATE RECOMMENDATIONS	☐	☐	☐	☐	☐	☐
SETS CLEAR STANDARDS AND HIGH EXPECTATIONS	☐	☐	☐	☐	☐	☐
REWARDS PERFORMANCE	☐	☐	☐	☐	☐	☐
ADVOCATES THE SHARING OF BEST PRACTICE	☐	☐	☐	☐	☐	☐
TACKLES POOR PERFORMANCE	☐	☐	☐	☐	☐	☐
PROVIDES TIMELY AND CONSTRUCTIVE CHALLENGE	☐	☐	☐	☐	☐	☐
SEES THE VALUE OF PERSONAL DEVELOPMENT	☐	☐	☐	☐	☐	☐

CHAPTER 5

Inner Strength

'He shows an ability to think clearly, remains composed in difficult situations and with awkward people. I feel he is just comfortable with himself.'

Covey, in 'The Seven Habits of Highly Effective People', suggests that private victories precede public ones, and that's what this cluster of behaviours is all about.[1] 'What lies behind us and what lies before us are but tiny matters compared to what lies within us.' Leading oneself is more than just knowing what lies within us. Leaders know not just what makes them tick, but also how to use that for the greater good of others. They understand thoroughly both their strengths and their weaknesses. That knowledge makes them more impactful.

The self-awareness of the most highly effective leaders is extremely accurate, which is unusual because the majority of leaders are ignorant of the strengths they have as well as the behaviours that impact negatively on others. My own research, which I share in Appendix 5, completely supports this. Hay Group research indicates that without self-awareness there's only a 17 per cent chance the leader can develop the social competencies such as customer focus and teamwork and a 4 per cent chance they can develop competencies around managing themselves, such as their achievement drive.[2]

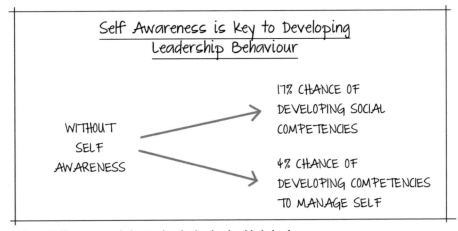

Fig 5.1 Self-awareness is key to developing leadership behaviour

Self-awareness is therefore the key to unlocking leadership potential. Such leaders are honest and at ease with themselves. You can spot this in the recruitment process; they are as comfortable talking about mistakes they have made as they are successes ... and usually with a grin on their face.

If self-awareness is a winning behaviour then self-deception is certainly a losing one.

In 'Leadership and Self Deception', the Arbinger Institute describe self-deception as undermining leadership ability.[3] They suggest that when leaders act contrary to their own values or beliefs, when they sense they should have done something but didn't, they are betraying themselves and putting themselves 'in the box'. Furthermore, once 'in the box' they suggest that leaders put a complexion on what they see to justify the act of self-betrayal. Being 'in the box' leaves leaders blind to the truth about themselves and others.

> Alex felt he had been passed over for promotion to a larger company in the Group. Despite the fact that he'd received feedback from the assessment centre, he couldn't believe that Jo had the job rather than himself. He'd been there longer, produced better results and always volunteered to help on Group-wide projects.
>
> Since that disappointment his colleagues have seen a changed man in Alex, openly disrespectful about everything Jo does and constantly alert for evidence to support his belief that the job should have been his.

When leaders get 'in the box', they see other people as someone to blame rather than to help. And with the focus on justifying leaders' own actions to themselves paramount, the focus on performance and results goes out of the window.

Only by being 'out of the box' can leaders see themselves and others for what they really are.

Leading self requires excellent self-awareness, coupled with the ability to manage that knowledge and impact favourably on others. Let's explore the components to leading self.

Leaders actively seek and are receptive to feedback

Not surprisingly, it starts with gathering information on leaders themselves. It's an obvious place to start but when we revisit our old friend the Johari window we can see so many reasons why movement from the blind spot to the public arena is less likely to happen for senior executives.[4]

We have already explored the range of emotions associated with the giving

Johari Window

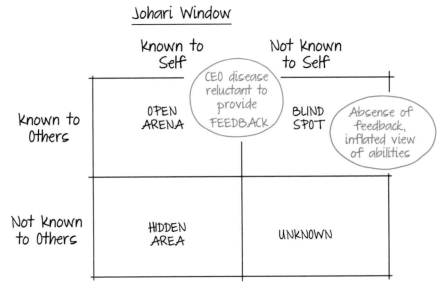

Fig 5.2 Johari window

and receipt of feedback in focus on performance. Jackman and Strober describe 'psychologically maladaptive behaviours such as procrastination, denial, brooding, jealousy and self-sabotage' as the way people typically respond to feedback.[5] They suggest that recognising these emotions and how you respond is critical to taking feedback on board and making plans to change, but that requires a high degree of self-awareness.

I believe that the higher up the hierarchy a leader is the more polarised these emotions become. It leads to what Goleman, Boyatzis and McKee refer to as the 'CEO disease'.[6] Direct reports are sometimes simply too scared to give anything other than positive feedback, perhaps wishing to avoid the response of some losing behaviours we'll discuss in the next chapter. Alternatively, they don't see that as their job. Where the feedback is about behaviour, some don't feel it's appropriate to share something so 'soft', although they feel with every interaction the very real impact it has on them. In summary, it feels uncomfortable giving feedback to senior people; there are very few upsides and plenty of downsides from the direct report's point of view.

And it gets worse when we look at how receptive senior leaders are. The absence of balanced feedback has left them with an inflated view of their abilities and behaviours. And why wouldn't it? They are living in a vacuum starved of the oxygen to develop behaviours that feedback provides. It becomes a vicious spiral:

the better you think you are and the more you demonstrate losing behaviours, the less chance you will receive feedback that reinforces your belief in the approach that has always worked ... and of course you are successful. Where's the need to change, even if you could? It's a sobering thought, but I'm convinced that the barriers to reducing leaders' blind spots simply increase with each rung on the career ladder they climb.

As if it could not get any worse, our blind spot is always the biggest pane (and opportunity) in the Johari window.[7] It's always larger than we think. The implications of a reluctance to provide feedback combined with unreceptive leaders means that, ironically, the blind spot will be largest for senior leaders at the very peak of the hierarchy.

The challenge for leaders is that, at best, feedback is going to be vague. Hence a specific approach is required to ferret out the important information they need to understand their relative strengths and weaknesses.

By welcoming feedback as a gift, leaders can demonstrate to others that they move through the transition denial to anger to acceptance quickly. They avoid behaviours such as brooding, procrastination, defensiveness and jealousy that simply put up barriers and discourage further gifts.

Leaders strong in this behaviour have a perceived openness that encourages the offer. An approach that embraces personal humility and humour softens the mood and encourages feedback; there's an absence of being defensive. In conversation with the leader others perceive that honesty is welcomed even when it is constructive criticism; it's regarded as completely acceptable. Openness and honesty are the keys to releasing offers of feedback. Conversations feel more comfortable as a result, even when discussing tough issues.

Leaders who actually do something with feedback encourage more. They express gratitude and, where appropriate, change or refine their behaviour. Leaders accept praise but are always on the look-out for ways to gather more insights about their behaviour and the impact it has.

'It's a pleasure to share feedback with him because of his attitude to addressing it: thorough and effective.'

After last year's performance review Kim has been focusing on only one aspect of behaviour. He had received clear feedback that he regularly took work off his team, in particular as deadlines approached. He'd done this with the best of intentions; he simply didn't want them to feel under pressure and, in any case, he'd put together more proposals than he cared to remember. He was just helping out and thought he was doing the right thing.

He didn't need to write a development plan; it was front of mind for him to 'stop taking work off my team'. He was convinced this would help with their development as well as his own. And Kim actually did it, for a whole year in spite of the fact that he was feeling extremely apprehensive about getting this year's feedback. He was convinced he had done what he'd planned but was far from convinced that it had worked, and in doing so he had felt extremely uncomfortable, as if it wasn't the right thing.

Once a leader has established a set of recurring behaviours, a way they feel comfortable leading, a way they feel is right, change is definitely possible but it feels awkward. This is just what Kim was experiencing: 'How can I possibly get better feedback when it's not felt "right" to me?'

Once a plan to change is made it's essential to get feedback, to check your behaviour has changed and to check that it's having the desired impact on others. Like anyone else, leaders need the feedback that a change in behaviour is working; it's encouragement that there's progress and, whilst it might feel a bit uncomfortable at the moment, there's plenty of comfort in the idea that others are perceiving it favourably. Getting comfortable with new leadership behaviours needs that reinforcement. It's a shame Kim waited a year to find out he'd been so successful.

One way to check whether you are getting quality feedback is to recall when the last time was that you got unprompted negative feedback, or how frequently you are challenged in team meetings. As the chair of a meeting you can gain insights by asking for feedback on the meeting itself. It's much easier for people to criticise a meeting than it is the leader. Listen attentively, record the comments and there will be some gems in there when you reflect and review later.

The perceptions of a leader's behaviour take time to change. When there are recurring themes and patterns that others have seen or experienced for many years, it requires resilience to focus constantly and visibly on a small number before others perceive a difference. Sometimes the improvement in subsequent performance reviews is slight, but it will gain momentum when a change in behaviours is persistently applied with the periodic check that the impact is positive. This is particularly true where the development plan is to reduce use of losing behaviours, where constant use has a more lasting impression. Don't be disappointed; it's the start of a journey.

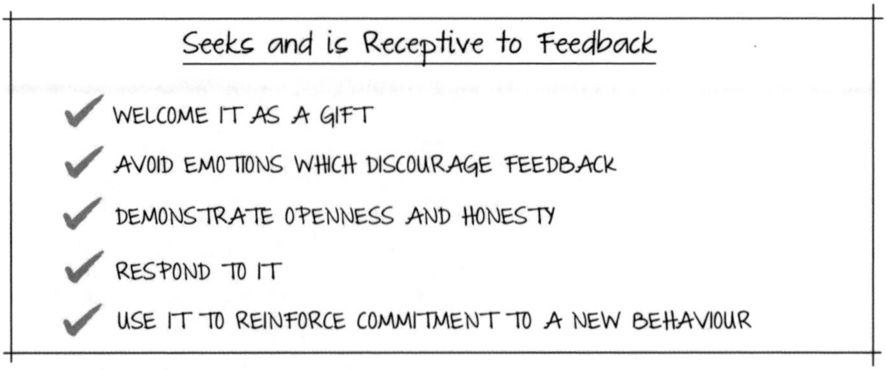

Seeks and is Receptive to Feedback

✔ WELCOME IT AS A GIFT

✔ AVOID EMOTIONS WHICH DISCOURAGE FEEDBACK

✔ DEMONSTRATE OPENNESS AND HONESTY

✔ RESPOND TO IT

✔ USE IT TO REINFORCE COMMITMENT TO A NEW BEHAVIOUR

Fig 5.3 Seeks and is receptive to feedback

Leaders accurately assess their strengths and weaknesses

Having received feedback to understand better their abilities and limits, leaders make the most of their knowledge. They are comfortable sharing it with others and, whilst confident, they seek help in areas where they consider themselves weak rather than falling short on the task.

This assessment comes with reflection, taking the time to work through the insights, feedback and observations you have picked up and making sense of them. Some leaders use a coach to help; others have their own personal way to contemplate. Sometimes it's more than reflection but challenging yourself: Am I making assumptions that constrain my leadership potential? What if I release the shackles of that assumption? And reflecting on a leader's values: If I behave consistently with who I believe I am, how would my leadership be different? Whichever approach you take, leaders make time for this process; they see it as a priority. From it comes a reassurance of leadership consistent with beliefs and as a result outward confidence.

An accurate assessment of relative strengths and weaknesses puts leaders in a very strong position. They are less likely to fail; they won't overstretch themselves because they know their relative strengths and when to seek help because they are equally aware of areas of weakness.

One of the leader's strengths is knowing his values and sharing them with others. Having the courage to live by those values is when other people around the leader perceive a sense of authenticity. Boyatzis, McKee and Goleman identify a number of signs for a leader that is no longer living according to their real self.[8] These are a sense of boredom, feeling trapped and a cry that 'life is too short'. With this, leaders feel their values are compromised and as leaders they are not completely comfortable with the way they act. When compromises are made and leaders do what they feel they ought to do, it's time for reflection away from the demands of work; time to rediscover the strength that is themselves and remain true to that.

Covey refers to this creation of time to reflect and assess as self-renewal and gives the following analogy of sharpening the saw that makes the point perfectly:

> Suppose you were to come upon someone in the woods working feverishly to saw down a tree.
> 'What are you doing?' you ask.
> 'Can't you see?' comes the impatient reply. 'I'm sawing down this tree.'
> 'You look exhausted!' you exclaim. 'How long have you been at it?'
> 'Over five hours,' he returns, 'and I'm beat! This is hard work.'
> 'Well, why don't you take a break for a few minutes and sharpen that saw?' you inquire. 'I'm sure it would go a lot faster.'
> 'I don't have time to sharpen the saw,' the man says emphatically. 'I'm too busy sawing!'[9]

Lencioni describes 'choosing invulnerability over trust' as a temptation to avoid.[10] Sharing a weakness or admitting a mistake is the greatest level of trust a leader can give; it puts their reputation and ego on the line. Lencioni suggests that 'in return (the leader) will get respect and honesty'.

Buckingham explains the secret of sustained individual success as focusing on your strengths.[11] There's an authenticity and confidence that is associated with a leader who constantly improves and refines behaviours or abilities where they are already strong. Indeed, Buckingham's advice is: 'The longer you put up with aspects of your work you don't like, the less successful you will be. So, as far as you are able, and as quickly as you can, stop doing them, and then see what the

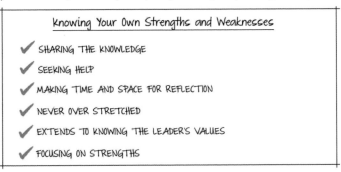

Fig 5.4 **Knowing your own strengths and weaknesses**

best of you, now focused and unfettered, can achieve.'

Personal motivation to change is required to 'undo' the old, ingrained habits and refine or replace them with new behaviours that have a more positive impact.

Leaders are aware of their personal triggers

They are acutely aware of the people and circumstances that annoy them. As a result, leaders prepare accordingly, either to overcome emotions or sometimes to use them to good effect. Being aware and open about their personal triggers also makes it easier for direct reports to manage their bosses. Leaders take time to analyse what causes their emotional response to build their understanding. They make clear how they are feeling: 'I'm frustrated by this' or 'I'm really excited by the idea, tell me more'. They are explicit about how they are feeling.

Once leaders are aware of their 'hot buttons' it becomes easier to ensure they don't impact either their decision making or their performance. It's an ongoing thing: during conversations and interactions the leader's mood changes just like anyone else's. The difference is that they spot the change and adapt appropriately, they self-regulate.

Goleman describes self-regulation as 'a propensity for reflection and thoughtfulness, comfort with ambiguity and change, and integrity – an ability to say no to impulsive urges'.[12]

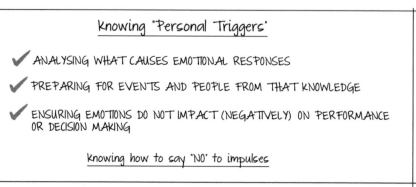

Fig 5.5 Knowing 'personal triggers'

Leaders channel their emotions to have a positive impact, ensuring they don't get in the way of action or decision making

On a practical level, leaders filter pressures on them from above to protect their direct reports. They take personal responsibility for how their team feels rather than blame something inherited from their own boss. But behaviourally and through their emotions they do much, much more than that.

Jones and Moorhouse suggest that pressure comes in two forms.[13] Some comes from the external environment leaders put themselves in consciously. Where leaders stand on the ring-toss is a good example of this, where they set their standards and goals. Alternatively, there is the internal pressure to perform leaders put themselves under, which can result in stress. 'Mentally tough performers have high self-awareness and the ability to regulate their thoughts, feelings, emotions and behaviour in a manner that delivers sustained success across a wide range of situations.'

Goleman, Boyatzis and McKee describe a mirroring process where the leader's emotions spread.[14] It's as if others 'catch the feelings'; it's infectious. When leaders channel their emotions they make the most of self-regulation and the fact that a leaders' moods are contagious.

Followers watch their boss; they look for any indication of mood, whether the door is open or closed, whether there's a smile or a frown, even the nuances in the daily greeting and the feelings behind the words that are spoken...or not. Everyone, including leaders, has an off day; they feel downbeat and grumpy. When they are on show, leaders manage it knowing the negative impact it will otherwise have on the motivation of others.

To demonstrate the behaviours associated with managing emotions a leader must be able to answer accurately the following questions, according to Kaplan.[15] 'What types of event create pressure for me? How do I behave under pressure? What signals am I sending my subordinates? Are these signals helpful, or are they undermining the success of my business?'

Leaders remain calm under pressure; their approachable, amicable and professional style does not waver when faced with the unforeseen or conflict; a respectful demeanour is maintained. Leaders do not panic or rush decisions where others react to what they perceive as the urgent need to do something. They remain engaged and involved no matter what pressure they are under, rather than let an emotional surge create an instantaneous knee-jerk reaction.

'She has been a stabilising force in the team in a difficult year. She is less likely to be influenced by what is going on around her. She simply accepts the challenge and quietly gets on with it.'

Leaders appear to take stock; they make time to reflect before choosing which response will have the best impact. Between stimulus and response everyone has the chance to consider options, but not all of us have that mental strength. Leaders don't feel rushed to respond; they will suspend their judgement until they have sought further views, listened and digested. They consider the impact on others and, in preparing for meetings, consider how they wish to come across. Leaders know when to be contemplative and when to speak up, even if it is uncomfortable. Perceived urgency hinders clear thinking and leaders are aware of this.

Leaders also appreciate that behaviour can be 'overdone'. They do get emotionally excited but know when and why it is happening and channel that enthusiasm constructively. They are seen as high-energy, involved and active people, but they seem to know when to tone that down and be more serious when the situation dictates. Similar to the theme we discussed when exploring the role intelligence plays in providing direction, emotions are managed here to ensure they do not appear overbearing. Leaders find the balance that ensures a high-performance culture without creating anxiety and stress.

Leaders use humour to good effect. Their sense of fun is infectious but again never overdone; they know when to apply it and equally when to stop. They use humour as a coping mechanism, when there's frustration or an impasse, for example. It takes nothing away from the situation, simply lightens the mood and encourages re-engagement. It takes the bite out of the situation without appearing less than professional.

Leaders laugh at themselves. They don't take themselves too seriously and will lift a group going through difficult times. It's the kind of humour that demonstrates that everyone, including leaders, is not always perfect, a degree of personal

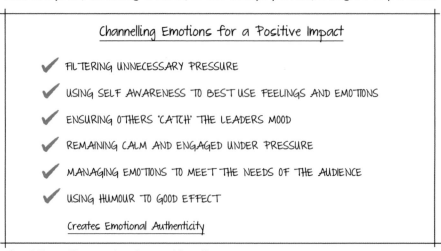

Fig 5.6 Channelling emotions for a positive effect

humility that's appreciated. Leaders take potentially uncomfortable situations and through injecting humour with reality move things forward.

Leaders appear genuine and sincere. There's an emotional authenticity, for example, they're moved when praising things that are important. They are not afraid to show they are annoyed but they do not let their emotions get in the way. Any anger is directed at the situation rather than the person.

We described authenticity, a leader knowing himself, as a strength. Goffee and Jones describe managing authenticity as the paradox of great leadership.[16] Leaders need to know their inner selves but in leading themselves to have the most positive impact on others will choose which traits to reveal to whom and when. They describe them as chameleons, adapting style to the needs of the person and situation without losing sight of who they are.

Leaders demonstrate confidence in themselves to perform

Rick Lash, in 'Top Leadership: Taking the Inner Journey', describes a part of that journey as 'facing the abyss', where leaders confront challenges that appear insurmountable: 'At pivotal moments in their careers, some leaders come face to face with feelings that have shadowed them all their lives including: self-doubt, fear of failure, not being heard and being left out.'[17]

Leaders conquer these moments without any outward signs. They create an appearance of self-assurance. From the feedback, this is perceived in two very different ways: firstly, what's described as boundless self-confidence – seeing every challenge and target as realistic – which transmits an optimistic feeling to others; and secondly, quiet confidence, involving leaders with clarity about direction who then just get on with things without fuss or fanfare. Whichever the perception, leaders radiate faith in themselves and their judgement.

There is a fine line to the behaviours at either extreme. On the one hand, they must ensure that boundless self-confidence does not tip into reckless decisions or targets that cannot be delivered; and on the other, quiet confidence must not

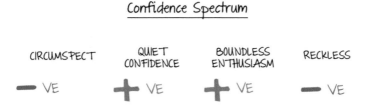

Fig 5.7 Confidence spectrum

lapse into appearing circumspect and unable to inspire.

Collins describes an element of 'level five leadership' as someone who 'acts with quiet, calm determination, and relies principally on inspired standards rather than inspiring charisma to motivate'.[18]

Leaders demonstrate self-confidence from a position based on personal beliefs and values. They are genuine, respectful and sensitive to others, but equally courageous to defend their convictions. That belief encourages them to take up the gauntlet without a safety net, such is their confidence. They don't avoid putting themselves at the edge of their comfort zone; their self-confidence is an intelligent and courageous one.

> *'He knows his qualities, having gone through legions of positive experiences, addicted to the pleasure of succeeding when challenged and armed with exceptional courage.'*

The extent of a leader's self confidence is the readiness and humility with which he admits mistakes, accepts that there are times when they simply 'don't know' and never blames anyone else or circumstances when things don't work out. When there's a doubt they are very open about it rather than covering up. This does not dent confidence in the leader; indeed, it generates respect. They act confidently without being overbearing, and are open to criticism and suggestions for improvement.

Admitting mistakes serves two other purposes: it disarms potential critics and it encourages others to do the same thing.

Collins describes another dimension of 'level five leadership' as someone who 'looks in the mirror, not out the window to apportion responsibility for poor results, never blaming other people, external factors or bad luck'.[19]

The head of IT is retiring and Chris feels that IT and Finance can be combined into one. He also feels he's the ideal candidate; in fact, the more he thinks about it the better the idea becomes. It will be Alex's decision, of course, but he'll sound out Fran first.

Whilst not discouraging Chris, Fran asks some pretty pertinent questions: 'This combined role implies stretching your leadership skills. What was your last set of data and feedback like?' Sadly not that great recalls Chris; he had forgotten that temporarily.

And then slightly more directly from Fran: 'Our organisation is growing quickly with both IT and Finance playing a key part. How do you propose explaining that you already have sufficient slack in your Finance role to take this on? And aren't you effectively saying the head of IT does so little you can pick it up as well?'

When he put it that way, Chris was glad he'd used Fran as a sounding board. At that moment he couldn't imagine how he'd come to the idea in the first place. It wasn't as if he didn't have enough to do and the head of IT was also working till all hours.

Sometimes misplaced 'over' confidence, where confidence shifts over the line, encourages leaders to see things through rose tinted glasses. They become lost in their own view of what is possible. Referring back to the last chapter on focus on performance, having a colleague to use as a sounding board is a great way to achieve a more balanced perspective before making a bold proposal.

Jones and Moorhouse describe self-belief as comprising two components: self-esteem and self-confidence. Self-esteem is how you see yourself. Leaders have a personal outlook on life; they are very clear about this and it consequently shapes their view on success or failure. Self-confidence comes from your perception of recent performances or experiences. It reflects leaders' relative optimism about the outcome. In summary, the combination of understanding yourself thoroughly and a track record of accomplishment (and learning from it) builds self-belief.

Finally, an encore from the Johari window: as a leader's confidence grows he is more likely to be more comfortable asking for information on his blind spots.[21] Someone who admits mistakes appears less defensive and the barriers to giving and receiving feedback fall.

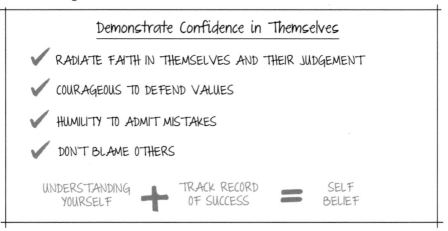

Fig 5.8 Demonstrate confidence in themselves

Leaders have a positive outlook; they are enthusiastic, energetic and show ambition
This behaviour is particularly contagious with those around the leader. It's an endearing quality that, when combined with an understanding of the business, instils confidence in others. Leaders are naturally enthusiastic about everything they are involved with; they see opportunities in one-to-ones with people rather than issues. A sense of 'we can do it' prevails and that attitude flows through to others

> *'Before we look at what's not working well for you,*
> *tell me about the highlights since we last met.'*

The combination of confidence and optimism helps leaders overcome barriers, partly because they see things in a positive light, as opportunities rather than hurdles, but also because of their approach. Leaders put in the extra effort.

> *'Despite them being a pain in the backside, at no*
> *time have I detected any reluctance from her to give*
> *anything other than 110% to resolving the matter.'*

Leaders chase stretching goals; they volunteer for anything that appears to be a challenge. They never appear daunted by a task. Even when tackling something new it is with the familiar gusto and enthusiasm. Leaders demonstrate energy and persistence in chasing what others would describe as crazy goals. Reflecting back to the ring-toss exercise, they are comfortable not only with a more stretching zone of creative tension but also with being at the top end of that as well. It's a level of optimism and confidence that despite the stretch still positively engages others.

Combining this optimistic outlook with the ability to match their mood to the people and situation around them is what makes some leaders very special.

Jones and Moorhouse describe how high performers make their motivation work for them.[22] Thinking back to the ring-toss exercise, they are not driven by fear of failure but by an anticipation of success – what they refer to as approach motivation rather than avoidance motivation.

Leaders are also aware of the biases that optimism and pessimism can create, both in themselves and in others. Lovallo and Kahneman explain how these biases work in 'Delusions of Success'.[23] One of the triggers is a general tendency for people to exaggerate their abilities, to believe themselves to be above average when, of course, half of us aren't. This is compounded by seeing things through rose tinted glasses, attributing success to things we've done ourselves and negative outcomes to basically anything else but ourselves. Finally, we tend to exaggerate the amount of control we have over circumstances, discounting chance or luck.

In business this optimistic bias is further stretched by accentuating the positives in a proposal and by failing to allow for a competitive response. As a result optimism can skew the business case.

> Sam has a proposal from a working group that has been thoroughly researched. They have also done sufficient sensitivity analysis to ascertain a range of outcomes. They propose the average, which shows benefits of 100 and costs of 40. Sam knows he will be competing for valuable resource and takes a more generous view on outcomes. Benefits of 110 are approved with costs of 34. A year later in a project review benefits of 56 and costs of 48 are reported. The key learning is that the project suffered because it clashed with the launch of another service initiative.

Does that sound familiar? Lovallo and Kahneman suggest 'anchoring' to balance that optimistic bias, essentially ascertaining whether a similar project has been undertaken either internally or externally.[24] The outcome of that is likely to be a safer prediction. They conclude that optimism does, however, have its place: 'it generates much more enthusiasm than it does realism but it enables people to be resilient when confronting difficult situations or challenging goals'.[25]

Having a Positive Outlook, Showing Enthusiasm

✓ HAVING THE CONFIDENCE AND OPTIMISM TO OVERCOME BARRIERS

✓ CHASING STRETCHING GOALS, VOLUNTEERING FOR CHALLENGES

✓ BEING AWARE OF THE BIAS OPTIMISM CAN CREATE

Instils confidence in others

Fig 5.9 Having a positive outlook, showing enthusiasm

Leading self requires a thorough understanding of your relative strengths and weaknesses, the insight to know which winning behaviours to apply under specific circumstances and with which people, and the emotional maturity to channel your values and feelings in a positive way. Throughout, a leader's authenticity, being true to themselves, is the source of inner strength.

What's your mechanism for raising self-awareness and getting a regular stream of quality feedback?

If you feel you are people oriented and empathetic but others see you as direct and task focused, whose perception impacts on performance?

Are you taking time out to assess your strengths and think through how your behaviour impacts others?

If moods are contagious, what feelings did you share today?

The impact on others of the behaviours associated with leading self is, firstly, a calming influence which encourages people to perform. This is a stark contrast to the unnecessary pressure we will see exerted through losing behaviours in the next chapter. Secondly, the confidence of the leader is transmitted to those around him, a confidence which also inspires others to do their best.

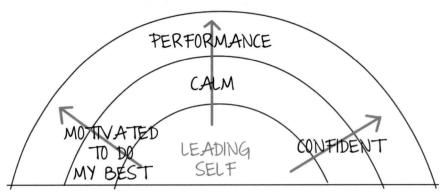

Fig 5.10 Links from leading self through impact on others to performance

Back to our diagnostic. If you are rating yourself strongly on the following, what evidence do you have for that assessment?

How often do you feel you demonstrate the behaviours associated with leading self?

How Characteristic are the Following for the Leader being Evaluated?

LEADING SELF

	NOT AT ALL		SOMEWHAT		VERY	DON'T KNOW
ACTIVELY SEEKS AND IS RECEPTIVE TO FEEDBACK	☐	☐	☐	☐	☐	☐
ACCURATELY ASSESSES THEIR OWN STRENGTHS AND WEAKNESSES	☐	☐	☐	☐	☐	☐
AWARE OF THEIR PERSONAL TRIGGERS	☐	☐	☐	☐	☐	☐
CHANNELS THEIR EMOTIONS TO HAVE A POSITIVE IMPACT	☐	☐	☐	☐	☐	☐
DEMONSTRATES CONFIDENCE IN THEMSELVES TO PERFORM	☐	☐	☐	☐	☐	☐
HAS A POSITIVE OUTLOOK, ENTHUSIASTIC, ENERGETIC AND SHOWS AMBITION	☐	☐	☐	☐	☐	☐

CHAPTER 6

The Dark Side

'He relies on his status to get things done rather than developing relationships to encourage others.'

My research included leaders who had left Belron® solely for performance reasons. This gives us the chance to contrast their behaviours with those of 'world class' executives. Interestingly, over half the feedback described an absence of winning behaviours but there was another group of leadership behaviours that had a negative impact on people around the leader. We'll call them losing behaviours.

First, let's look at how people described what it is like when the winning behaviours we have explored in the last four chapters are missing. It's a good way to recap and appreciate why they are so impactful.

When providing direction is missing:

'Freedom to act is fine but it needs some guidance, where we fit into the wider business is not always clear.'

'Fails to see which battles are worth fighting.'

'She does not buy in to what we are doing and tries to delay progress from inactivity on her behalf.'

When engagement is missing:

'He does not realise that others may have a different perspective. The world is not black and white.'

'He holds back information unless you specifically ask for it.'

'She needs to match her delivery to the audience if she wants participation.'

'I can see in his body language what he is really thinking but he says something completely different.'

When focus on performance **is missing:**

'You get the sense the team are craving more support and guidance.'

'He's light on feedback to his team, more focused on the task.'

'He sets goals which are more inspirational than calculated. It leads to a lack of credibility.'

'He's been tolerant of poor performers. He's just not close enough to it.'

When leading self **is missing:**

'He tries to extend his influence beyond his own department but it comes across as self-promotion.'

'His "air of superiority" makes it difficult to discuss and resolve issues.'

'She asked for feedback, which I gave, then she immediately started to justify it, leaving me with the feeling that I had gained nothing by being honest.'

'His interpersonal skills are awful, inflaming things rather than making any attempt at a sensible conversation.'

The Dark Side

When PROVIDING DIRECTION is missing:

✗ UNCLEAR WHERE PEOPLE FIT IN

✗ LACK OF FOCUS

✗ NO BUY-IN

When ENGAGEMENT is missing:

✗ SEE THINGS AS BLACK AND WHITE

✗ HOARDING INFORMATION

✗ INCONSIDERATE OF OTHERS

✗ LACK OF AUTHENTICITY

When FOCUS ON PERFORMANCE is missing:

✗ ABSENCE OF SUPPORT AND FEEDBACK

✗ SETTING UNATTAINABLE GOALS

✗ TOLERANCE OF MEDIOCRITY

When LEADING SELF is missing:

✗ SELF PROMOTION

✗ ARROGANCE

✗ DEFENSIVE

✗ AGGRAVATES THE SITUATION

Fig 6.1 When winning behaviours are missing

The Losing Behaviours

Firstly, there's a lack of Winning Behaviours
(Over half the feedback)

Fig 6.2 An absence of winning behaviours

Lack of a sense of direction, lack of a degree of engagement around the individual and task, lack of conversations on how to improve performance, and having a boss who fails to appreciate the impact of his emotions on others all leave people drifting aimlessly, at best feeling unwanted, at worst bearing the brunt of their boss's moods.

That's how an absence of winning behaviours from a boss feels; and, if that's not enough, for some people it's compounded by another set of 'losing behaviours'.

Let's look at the losing behaviours leaders should avoid, which represent the other half of the feedback comments on leaders.

Leaders tell or show others what to do

This is the largest cluster of feedback on losing behaviours.

Telling takes a number of forms. At one extreme it's shouting others down to make a point that the leader expects to be followed. At the other extreme it's being polite, with lots of 'pleases' and 'thank yous', but the real gist of the conversation is the leader expecting you to follow his instructions as quickly as possible. 'You know what happened to the last person who didn't do it this way? I wouldn't like the same to happen to you.'

Both routes are direct, and both routes tend to avoid dialogue – after all, it's a waste of valuable time. One just feels a bit 'softer' than the other. There's an assumption that the leader's time is the most important; they call meetings and expect others to drop everything to be there. It's a well-worn phrase but there's an impression that 'it's the boss's way or no way'. There's also a sense that if there's a dialogue it is more an argument or directive than a debate.

In terms of share of voice, leaders talk far more than they listen and at the extreme don't allow anyone to interject whilst they are talking, even though the audience know the rest of the monologue will add nothing. Additionally, they will talk over others to ensure they get their point across. Leaders can give the perception that control is the best way to get things done, for example controlling key messages, hoarding information and avoiding empowerment.

It's tempting to think these leaders are nasty people with a poor outlook, but that's not necessarily true. We are not talking about personality here but the behaviours others see from the leader. If the leader genuinely and sincerely believes that the only way to get things done is as quickly as possible then what others see is a demand for immediate compliance. Irrespective of how that is perceived by others it is well intentioned from the leader's point of view – to them that's the way to get results.

Let's move on to leadership by showing.

Leaders who lead by showing give the perception that standards are everything, specifically the standards of the leader. They will take tasks or responsibilities away from others and hold on to detailed tasks because leaders feel they are not meeting their own high standards. Certain activities they will guard jealously.

Leaders like to front and deliver presentations, even when the rest of their team are present. They are highly critical of work that does not come up to scratch, which comes across as negative in the absence of any balancing praise.

In summary, leading by showing involves a leader doing literally anything to get the outcome they desire. They believe there's a certain way to get tasks done and become overbearing in ensuring that standard is delivered.

'She will push too far and attempt to take control of things that are someone else's responsibility in her drive to get the outcome she would like.'

A leadership approach that tells or shows is very common. It comes naturally to people who feel things need to be done quickly and to high standards. They instinctively feel it's the way to get things done: what other way is there? In that sense results are delivered with the best of intent but there are two big issues with it. First is the impact on others and second is that leaders become blind to this and their leadership behaviour in general.

Taking the impact on others first. Goleman describes the tell and show behaviours as the Hay Group coercive and pacesetting styles respectively.[1] The coercive style leaves people 'unable to act on their own initiative'; there's a complete absence of empowerment. The pacesetting style is overwhelming, sometimes described as the 'heart attack' style both for the leader delivering it as well as those on the receiving end. A key impact of winning behaviours is to feel trusted; that's eliminated with this style because everything revolves around the leader's standards.

With regard to self-awareness I researched leaders who were dominant (a recurring leadership behaviour, one frequently observed by others) in only one of the Hay Group leadership styles. In other words they led in only one way. This is summarised in Appendix 9. For the groups that tell or show, all thought they were not using that style to the same degree. They grossly underestimated their strength in telling or showing. They were effectively blind to the style they were using and the consequent impact on others.

But it got worse, for not only were they blind to the dissonant style they were using but 85 per cent felt they were using the resonant styles associated with the winning behaviours when in fact these styles were not seen by others. This represents a serious challenge for leaders blighted in this way: they just don't see the corrosive impact losing behaviours have on others. The combination of the behaviour with the impact it has on others means that leaders are unlikely to get the feedback they need. That's a bad combination of circumstances. Getting quality feedback on losing behaviours in a form that builds awareness is critical. In my experience it's seldom solved without an intermediary or coach to help with the process ... There are just too many barriers for a leader to appreciate their impact on their own.

Can you imagine a leader seeking examples to gain understanding and self-awareness when their natural leadership styles are losing behaviours? Remember that their drivers are immediate compliance and high standards, so the request for insights will be demanding, urgent and in great detail. 'Thanks for the feedback but no one's leaving the room until we've got to grips with this. I need a list of examples from each of you.'

Goleman, Boyatzis and McKee describe the impact of the tell approach as follows: 'If a leader's out of control outbursts go hand in hand with a lack of empathy, an emotional tone deafness, the style can run amok. The dictatorial leader barks orders, oblivious to the reactions of people on the receiving end.'[2] And of the show approach: 'The most glaring lack is emotional self-management, a deficit that manifests itself as either micromanaging or impatience or worse.[3]

> It was getting close to the date for the annual budget presentation to Group. It was just a week away and whilst the story was in good shape some of the numbers still did not stack up. Despite several conversations between Alex and Chris, Alex was starting to get frustrated and concerned that it was not going to be ready on time. On Friday evening he said, 'Don't worry, Chris, give me the spreadsheets and I'll work on them over the weekend.' Alex even added, 'I know it's wrong; I just can't help it. After all, it's my first budget as a general manager. I know you won't mind.'

The temptation is great and sadly it's a familiar story. You sometimes see it with sales directors who delegate responsibility for the presentation to their team only to take it back and finish off as the meeting with the key account approaches and they become anxious. Such actions have a profound impact on others: 'How does Chris feel about his spreadsheet being taken away, when it's his job?' The perception is 'I've failed' and 'He doesn't trust me.'

Let's take another perspective on the tell approach to leadership.

> Nicky likes the concept of different leadership behaviours or approaches for different people, what is sometimes called situational leadership. It's an element of 'engagement', one of the ways leaders build rapport and emotional commitment, and he's pleased that he does this himself. He's always believed that long servers in his team should be given more freedom because they have 'learnt the ropes'. New people, however, require much more hand-holding and closer management until they have 'earned their stripes'.
>
> He's about to recruit a new team member in an assessment centre with Fran and proudly explains how he manages people differently. Fran's answer completely takes the wind out of his sails: 'Why are you recruiting someone you need to tell what to do? Why don't you recruit someone who prefers a discussion on where we are going and then empower him to get on with it?' Despite his delight in being able to adapt his leadership approach Nicky wondered where the losing behaviour feedback was coming from and felt he had something to work on.

Any leader's job is to manage a talented group of individuals; it is certainly not to tell any of them what to do. Their role is to explain why the vision or priorities are so important; not to share detailed steps on how to get there. There is evidence that when leaders persistently use a tell approach then followers become accustomed to wanting less autonomy. Consequently, it's the last behaviour you want to be role-modelling to a new employee. You don't want to create a first impression akin to 'command and control'.

Leaders sometimes create an environment that plays to their natural behaviours. Take, for example, a general manager who creates endless lists of priorities, tasks and initiatives that they allocate to their team with strict deadlines. It's overload because they already have day jobs to do, so what happens? The team take the only course open to them and make an appointment to see the general manager for his view and the quick answer, he tells or shows, and his natural style comes to the rescue yet again! When we explored 'providing direction' in Chapter 2 we discussed the importance of making priorities clear. Long lists imply a lack of clarity on what really matters and are often a reflection on the prevailing style of the boss.

There is a big flaw in a behaviour that requires leaders to tell or show. It requires the leader to be involved or physically there, as opposed to an empowered approach where tasks and decisions are delegated with confidence. The leader becomes the constraint because everything has to go through them. In large, widely dispersed organisations that approach simply can't work efficiently or effectively. There's arrogance in the assumption behind tell and show suggesting that leaders actually know best or have higher standards.

As if that is not enough, research shared in 'Coaching for Performance' by Whitmore indicates that tell and show styles are poor approaches to learning.[4] It's the experience that comes from empowerment supported by coaching that has the biggest sustained impact.

Impact of Tell, Show and Experience on Recall

	TOLD	TOLD AND SHOWN	TOLD, SHOWN AND EXPERIENCED
RECALL AFTER 3 WEEKS	70%	72%	85%
RECALL AFTER 3 MONTHS	10%	32%	65%

Fig 6.3 Impact of tell, show and experience on recall

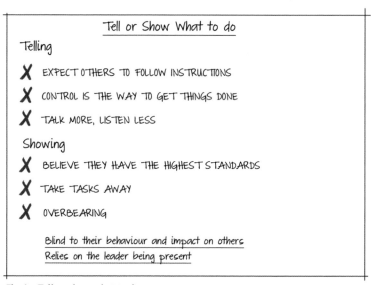

Tell or Show What to do

Telling

✗ EXPECT OTHERS TO FOLLOW INSTRUCTIONS

✗ CONTROL IS THE WAY TO GET THINGS DONE

✗ TALK MORE, LISTEN LESS

Showing

✗ BELIEVE THEY HAVE THE HIGHEST STANDARDS

✗ TAKE TASKS AWAY

✗ OVERBEARING

Blind to their behaviour and impact on others
Relies on the leader being present

Fig 6.4 Tell or show what to do

Whilst 'tell and show' leadership represented the largest cluster of feedback, there are other losing behaviours that we should be aware of.

Leaders avoid contact with others, operating in a silo

One of the stark contrasts between winning and losing behaviours is the use of the words 'open' and 'closed' respectively in the feedback comments. It was a recurring theme.

They operate within their own part of the organisation. Leaders are reluctant to get involved elsewhere and shun input also. As a result they are described as insular in their approach. The absence of a network means there's an absence of communication with important stakeholders and consequently key messages don't get through.

Contact in general is kept to a minimum. If there's consultation the leader is presumed by others to reflect on it but no one hears anything back. No one really knows if input has been considered or taken into account. Eventually people work around the leader; they will get the information they need from elsewhere, often from the leader's team themselves.

'If you don't contact him, he won't contact you' is typical of such leaders. They are difficult to meet, often late for meetings, reserved and in particular described as leaving their teams at crucial moments.

The lack of contact means that managers working for these leaders are unclear on the authority invested in them, simply because there has been no dialogue. This causes confusion all round.

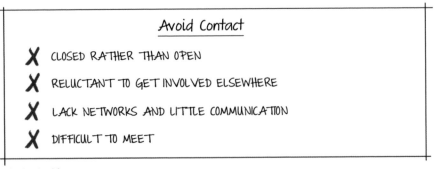

Fig 6.5 Avoid contact

Leaders appear inflexible, defensive and risk averse

They appear closed to alternative ways of doing things, usually making decisions that rely upon their own previous experience. Leaders appear to view things as black and white, my way or no way.

They either do not ask for, or worse, ask but do not listen to other people's points of view; hence they come across as having very set ideas. It leaves others feeling as if the decision has already been made, the leader having preconceived ideas. It's all the more frustrating if there's a 'false' debate where the outcome feels preordained.

> 'Tends to do his thinking and planning in advance. It can then be difficult to influence his view once he has made his mind up.'

Leaders focus on their own agenda

They spend a lot of time on the tasks they enjoy and either shy away from or delegate the activities they find stressful or difficult.

Leaders spend time promoting themselves, whether that's pandering to their own boss, taking praise due to others or hiding their own mistakes. By focusing on themselves they appear to take themselves too seriously, especially in large groups; or they are seen as arrogant, feeling a need to show people what they have done or what they know.

The focus on themselves leaves leaders blind to the bigger picture. They are literally not aware of things that could impact the leader's part of the organisation or of the problems others have. Calling impromptu meetings, described as urgent, without checking everyone's diary is a good example of this self-focus. There's no concern for anyone else.

> 'It's important to him, therefore we all need to clear our schedules to be there.'

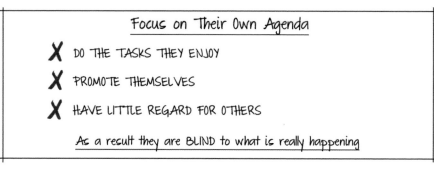

Focus on Their Own Agenda

✗ DO THE TASKS THEY ENJOY

✗ PROMOTE THEMSELVES

✗ HAVE LITTLE REGARD FOR OTHERS

As a result they are BLIND to what is really happening

Fig 6.6 Focus on their own agenda

Leaders get immersed in detail

*'To get the level of detail he needs he'll ask
three people the same question.'*

It sometimes seems as if they are anxious to gather more data when the big picture is abundantly clear to everyone else. They commit a huge amount of personal time to reviewing, fastidiously checking every detail. This is perceived as being overly cautious in decision making. A craving for the complete picture means that opportunities are missed or benefits reduced by the delay.

When leaders respond in great detail, it's frustrating, particularly if others have already acknowledged they understand. Further explanation feels laboured and pedantic, and motivation sags. Others start to switch off.

Sometimes it's the task itself that is the detail. Leaders get involved in decisions that, quite frankly, others are more capable of making, and indeed are actually responsible for making.

*'He asks to check my communications before they
go out, puts ridiculous limits on purchasing and even
decides what biscuits we'll have for the meeting.'*

Leaders who are immersed in detail fail to see the impact on others and invariably miss deadlines, resulting in a general lack of commitment to people and task.

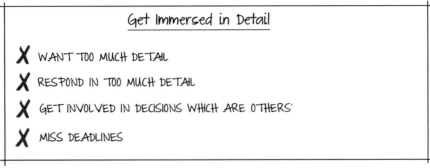

Fig 6.7 Get immersed in detail

Leaders express frustration with others and events

This frustration usually comes from a desire to get on with task, so things like communication and meetings just get in the way; they are an irritation. Frustration is shared with whoever happens to be around: 'he never holds back'. Alternatively, the frustration is about work that fails to meet the leader's expectations or standards.

> 'She cannot disguise her feelings when
> someone falls short of expectations.'

With this behaviour there's a sense that the leader is not approachable, certainly not with news the leader may not want to hear. If a discussion or debate is not going the way the leader anticipated, their body language becomes immediately apparent. When things go wrong it's everyone's fault but their own; they will even blame the organisation's culture itself.

The impact of the behaviour, whether that is open criticism, assigning blame or quickly dismissing any alternative view, is a lack of respect for others.

Collins describes leaders in organisations who are grasping for salvation: 'instead of being calm, deliberate and disciplined, people exhibit hasty reactive behaviour bordering on panic'.[5] And Goleman, Boyatzis and McKee encourage leaders to 'drive the collective emotions in a positive direction and clear the smog created by toxic emotions'.[6]

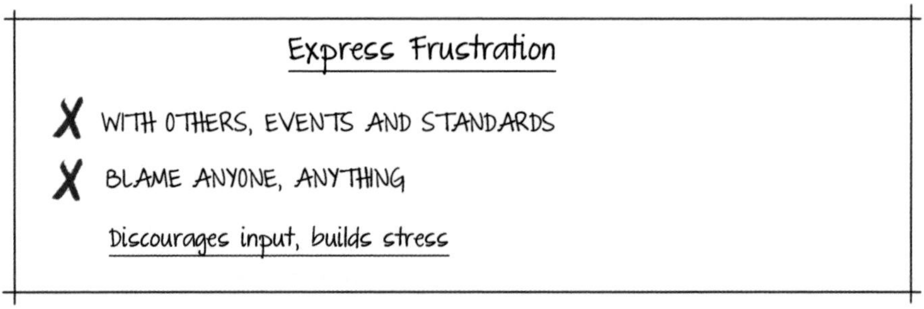

Fig 6.8 Express frustration

Spreier, Fontaine and Malloy describe the impact of a high achievement motive on leadership behaviour.[7] Unchecked, they are the losing behaviours I've described, a tendency to command and control, and absence of communication and trust. They suggest that, whilst the solution is obvious, 'less coercive, more collaborative' and 'influence rather than direct', it's surprising that executives resort to the same behaviour time and again. 'They don't just know achievement is important, they feel it. Achievement is a natural high for them.'

Achievement has its virtues. The relevance to us is directing it appropriately as a winning rather than a losing behaviour. It's the management of emotions we discussed in leading self.

LaFasto and Larson created the following checklist to assess the behaviours of high control leaders:

Does the team leader only try to give the illusion of gathering input?

Does the team leader limit the discussion by cutting it off while team members feel there is still more to say?

Do team members ever feel hoodwinked or manoeuvred into a decision?

Does the team leader usually get annoyed when discussions dig into the issues, referring to the discussions as a waste of time?

Does the team leader try to prescribe the taste or style of others?

Does the team leader seem negative and overly critical of things in general?

Does the team leader get unnecessarily immersed in details that could be entrusted to team members?

Does the team leader make others feel defensive?

Do team members feel they have to position a topic just right in order to avoid an abrupt halt to a discussion or being handed a solution?[8]

It's a great list for self-reflection on traits to avoid. A side effect of controlling behaviour is that it is self-reinforcing. The absence of feedback and the sense they are making the right calls just encourages these leaders to carry on regardless of the impact their behaviour has on others.

Leaders can relapse

Leaders who become comfortable with winning behaviours and demonstrate them regularly can slip dramatically into losing behaviours. Ironically, one of the reasons is promotion, owing to a combination of the need to impress a new boss, create a quick win and urgently fill the void the vacancy left. Losing behaviours offer 'route one': the natural instincts that have been managed positively by the leader in their previous role and one of the reasons they achieved the promotion lapse. Leading by either telling or showing prevails once more. The winning behaviours of providing direction, and engagement, focusing on performance and leading yourself will always achieve better results in the long term.

This quote is typical from those working with a leader who demonstrates losing behaviours:

'He tries to involve us but as soon as he's under stress he just reverts to type. Then he just gives the perception that he doesn't need a team at all.'

Van Buren and Safferstone identify five traps to avoid on the way to a quick win.[9] They are: focusing too heavily on detail, reacting negatively to criticism, intimidating others, jumping to hasty conclusions, and micromanaging direct reports. It's a very good summary of the losing behaviours.

Tackling self-awareness

Because of the 'blindness' associated with the behaviours (Appendix 9) the development issues for leaders are building self-awareness about the extent to which losing behaviours are employed before moving on to change the behaviour.

Anonymous feedback is likely to be more accurate, so feedback based on a diagnostic (Appendix 20) where responses are averaged is a good option. Alternatively a trusted third party, perhaps a coach, can interview people around the leader with the commitment to feedback themes rather than specific examples. Talking with a coach about recent leadership conversations can help. A good coach will spot behaviours and ask incisive questions to build understanding. Finally gaining feedback on meetings chaired by the leader may give some clues; talking about the meeting process rather than the leader himself will be easier for others.

The irony is that good leaders, those using winning behaviours, are likely to get more and better quality feedback. It's back to that contrast between appearing open rather than closed. For leaders demonstrating losing behaviours it's a question of being patient, usually a trait they don't possess, and working with what data they can gather.

Transforming losing to winning behaviours

Turning losing behaviours into winning behaviours is surprisingly easy once the leader has gained awareness of the behaviours they are using. Let's assume that the leader is aware of the behaviours they are using and has a desire to change.

We'll take some common phrases from leaders who tell and with a slight finesse transform them into the winning behaviour providing direction:

'I'll tell you what you are going to do'
becomes
'I'll explain why our strategy is so important.'

'We are pushed for time so I'll just tell you what to do'
becomes
*'We are pushed for time so let's remind
ourselves of our priorities.'*

'This is what your team needs to do'
becomes
*'How can your team best support our
vision over the coming months?'*

And *'It's really important that you get on with this straight away'*
becomes
*'Because it's key to delivering our strategy, speed
is important; let me know how I can help?'*

In each example it's a few words that change the perceived behaviour and also the impact it has on others.

Let's have a look at the phrases a leader who shows might use and change these into the winning behaviour focus on performance:

'Why don't you watch me and then you will know what to do?'
becomes
*'Why don't I watch you do it and then I
can give you some feedback?'*

'I've an idea you should try'
becomes
'Tell me what ideas you have got?'

'This is what I would do'
becomes
'What would you do?'

And *'This is my standard'*
becomes
'What are your goals?'

Phrases associated with both tell and show styles of leadership can so easily be amended and the impact on others transformed.

In 'Outliers', Gladwell explains why Korean Air had such a poor safety record.[10] It was partly attributed to cultural differences. Hofstede's Cultural Dimensions Power Distance Index measures the extent to which the less powerful members of organisations and institutions (like the family) accept and expect that power is distributed unequally; in other words a deference to hierarchy where an attitude to command and control could be considered acceptable.[11] The captain did not expect to be questioned and the crew had no intention of questioning his decisions.

What's relevant for us is not so much that cultural differences can explain an approach to management, but the solution. Korean Air could have employed people of different nationalities but instead trained Koreans to manage their cultural instincts in the interests of safety. It's the same for leadership: everyone is predisposed to a certain approach to leadership that feels natural to them. No one expects an individual to change their personality but what is reasonable is to expect an individual to learn how to manage behaviours that have a negative impact on people around them when leading.

There's one final comment I would like to make about losing behaviours. If your boss uses them regularly and you experience the impact, that's not an excuse to pass that style on to your own team. As a leader in your own right, you are responsible for demonstrating winning behaviours with those around you. There is no opt-out clause. For example, just because you are unclear on direction it is no excuse for failing to create it for others. It's more of a challenge, admittedly, but it remains your job.

The main impact of losing behaviours is that others feel unnecessary pressure to perform; they feel stressed rather than stretched. And as a result performance suffers.

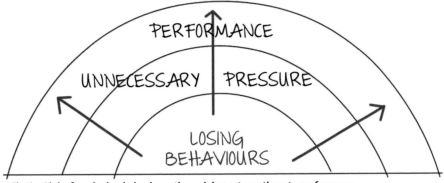

Fig 6.9 Links from losing behaviours through impact on others to performance

Returning to our diagnostic, this time these are behaviours to avoid. How do you feel others would respond to the questions about you?

How Characteristic are the Following
for the Leader being Evaluated?

LOSING BEHAVIOURS	NOT AT ALL		SOMEWHAT		VERY	DON'T KNOW
TELLS OR SHOWS OTHERS WHAT TO DO	☐	☐	☐	☐	☐	☐
AVOIDS CONTACT WITH OTHERS AND OPERATES IN A SILO	☐	☐	☐	☐	☐	☐
APPEARS INFLEXIBLE, DEFENSIVE AND RISK AVERSE	☐	☐	☐	☐	☐	☐
FOCUSES ONLY ON THEIR OWN AGENDA	☐	☐	☐	☐	☐	☐
GETS IMMERSED IN DETAIL	☐	☐	☐	☐	☐	☐
EXPRESSES FRUSTRATION WITH OTHERS AND EVENTS	☐	☐	☐	☐	☐	☐

CHAPTER 7

The Winning Feeling

In this chapter we'll look at how it feels to be on the receiving end of winning behaviours. When we discussed the quality of feedback earlier you may recall that the very best feedback describes both what someone sees or feels and the impact it has on them and others. The winning feeling is the impact on others experiencing winning behaviours. It's the critical link between a leader's behaviour and a desired outcome or result.

Fig 7.1 Links from winning behaviours through impact on others to performance

The following matrix, overleaf, summarises the links between aspects of leadership behaviour and the impact felt by others.

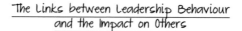

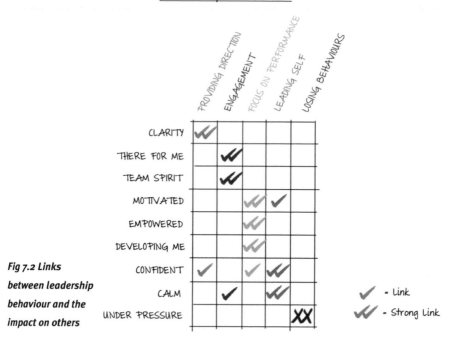

Fig 7.2 Links between leadership behaviour and the impact on others

Let's have a look in more detail at the impact winning behaviours have on others.

I have the clarity required to do my best

This comes exclusively from the providing direction behaviours. Clarity is achieved through various routes. For some, clarity is achieved by constant reinforcement of priorities and reassurance that the vision is something worthy of effort.

> 'Never lets a conversation go by without some insightful observation on customer service and he consistently delivers that message every time he presents.'

For others, a dialogue that helps explain where they fit in creates clarity based on the fact that a leader can explain simply the links between vision and day-to-day tasks.

> 'The rigour of thought that goes into the vision provides clarity and comfort to the audience that the links are clearly understood.'

When clarity is missing, the biggest impact is uncertainty and the leader's decision-making ability comes into question. People don't understand what's required of them or how they can make a contribution that is valued. It's the feeling Lencioni describes as 'irrelevance' in 'The Three Signs of a Miserable Job'.[1] People need to see a connection between their work and the 'big picture' to gain fulfilment.

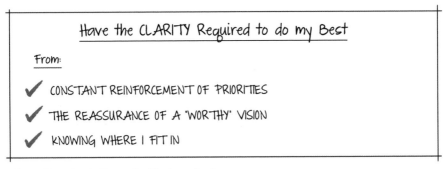

Fig 7.3 Have the clarity required to do my best

I feel he cares about me; we've an open and trusting relationship (there for me)

Lencioni describes another sign of a miserable job as 'anonymity'.[2] 'People who see themselves as invisible, generic or anonymous cannot love their jobs.'

Being 'there for me' represented the greatest volume by way of feedback comments on the impact of leadership behaviour, almost a third of the total. Both Kouses and Posner,[3] and O'Toole and Bennis[4] describe trust and honesty as the most sought after values in a leader, so perhaps we should not be surprised.

The driver here is the behaviour associated with engagement. People feel leaders are sensitive to their feelings because of the way leaders target messages to be meaningful on a personal level. They value a leader who makes himself available to listen and who welcomes the views of others. There's a sense of trust that people find motivating.

'He creates exceptional proximity and trust, someone with whom you feel familiar and at ease.'

Human values such as sharing and caring, a sense that people are important, create a positive energy. It's the openness (as opposed to the closed nature associated with losing behaviours) that makes a difference.

Leaders avoid conducting themselves politically, which is greatly appreciated.

Equality, fairness and valuing diversity are attributes that demonstrate openness.

Trust supports other elements of the working environment that are appreciated. Horovitz with Ohlsson-Corboz propose that a combination of trust and stretch increases self-confidence, and that a combination of trust and support encourages collaboration and teamwork.[5]

An environment in which people feel trust as part of the culture encourages quality feedback to reduce blind spots and the sharing of personal insights to reduce the private arena. Openness, characterised by a large public arena in the

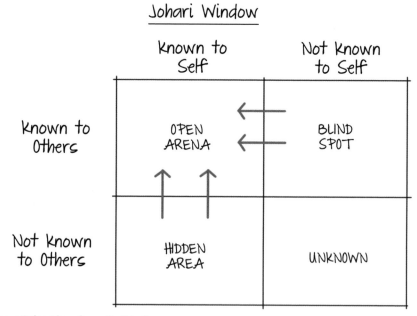

Fig 7.4 Being 'there for me' builds the open area

Johari window, becomes a way of life and is greatly appreciated.[6]

Machin describes the role of trust when coaching.[7] To explore beneath the surface, at what he calls 'psychological depth', requires a coach to build and maintain a trusting relationship. Machin proposes that the leader as coach should exhibit high levels of empathy, demonstrate a non-judgemental approach, listen with rapt attention and be honest, open and congruent. With regard to the relationship itself he suggests that leaders work at the appropriate level of psychological depth, build trust and rapport, hold people to account, and provide time and space and the appropriate level of challenge.

TRUST is a key Part of the Leader as
Coach Relationship

From:

✔ EMPATHY

✔ LISTENING

✔ NON-JUDGEMENTAL APPROACH

✔ HONESTY, AUTHENTICITY

✔ PROVIDING TIME AND SPACE

✔ PSYCHOLOGICAL DEPTH (not just a business discussion)

✔ THE RIGHT AMOUNT OF SUGGESTION

✔ A BALANCE BETWEEN SUPPORT AND CHALLENGE

Fig 7.5 Trust is a key part of the leader as coach relationship

In contrast, trust is absent where losing behaviours are employed. When trust is not felt it's often a result of a leader appearing reluctant to move forward or holding on to tasks and information. Alternatively, lack of trust comes from arrogance or open disrespect for others.

Galford and Drapeau trace a breakdown of trust to inconsistent messages, inconsistent standards, misplaced benevolence, false feedback, a failure to trust others and failure to tackle the issues everyone is talking about behind closed doors.[8] They also point out that 'distrust thrives in a vacuum' where there's a lack of information.

Galford and Drapeau recommend steps to rebuild trust. First, work out what happened and whether loss of trust was reciprocal. They suggest that, whilst it's normal to be angry when trust is betrayed, retaliation is not an option. Second, assess the depth of the breakdown in trust, then acknowledge the issue and your commitment to address it. Finally, identify what needs to be done and get on with it.

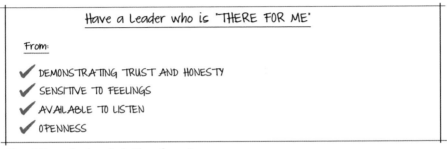

Have a Leader who is "THERE FOR ME"

From:

✔ DEMONSTRATING TRUST AND HONESTY

✔ SENSITIVE TO FEELINGS

✔ AVAILABLE TO LISTEN

✔ OPENNESS

Fig 7.6 Have a leader who is 'there for me'

I feel a sense of team spirit

This comes predominantly from engagement behaviours. There's a sense of pride in the way the team works and what they achieve together. Energy is not wasted on internal politics; it is focused on building trust within the team. There's a discussion culture where everyone's opinion counts, which enriches the team and pushes the boundaries. Openness creates great team dynamics and humour keeps spirits high.

Even where a team is widely dispersed, 'togetherness' remains. People feel proud to work in the team and motivated to make a contribution. Everyone feels valued.

'People relish opportunities to demonstrate
to others what this team can do.'

There's an investment of time together to build a team spirit that delivers better results as a consequence.

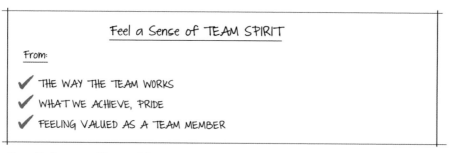

Fig 7.7 Feel a sense of team spirit

I feel motivated and inspired to do my best work

The biggest contributor here comes from the behaviours associated with focusing on performance. Praise and encouragement play a big part. The leader always demonstrates excitement and passion around the achievements and progress made by others. That enthusiasm is contagious; there's a feeling that the leader brings out the best in people. This motivation comes from a focus on the positive aspects of what is happening.

'He is very quick to praise and encourage progress. He
leaves me with the feeling I can achieve my goals.'

High standards also make a difference; they are motivating and create a positive energy. Striving to achieve realistic and stretching standards is linked to a positive learning experience. The ring-toss exercise we explored in Chapter 4 explains how this excitement comes when leaders engage with people around their zone of creative tension.

> *'An absolute compulsion to provide excellent*
> *service which is highly motivating encourages*
> *me to turn in a very good performance.'*

The inspiration also comes from a leader's ability to manage themselves; their emotional behaviour triggers others to 'go for it'. Forward and positive thinking leaders are exciting to be around.

> *'He transmits an optimistic feeling to his team*
> *who deliver results; it's a reflection on him.'*

Finally, it's no coincidence that inspired work is linked to clarity about its making a difference.

Fig 7.8 Feel motivated, inspired to do my best

I feel empowered and accountable

It's interesting that people value both empowerment and a leader 'being there' for them; it's further evidence that to be effective leaders need to understand where that balance is for each individual they work with.

The feelings of empowerment and responsibility originate from discussions with the leader using the 'focusing on performance' behaviours.

'He lets you get on with your job with minimum intervention.
However, I always know he is there in the background
keeping an eye on things, which is reassuring.'

Empowerment with accountability from a leader who delegates with confidence is a liberating and positive experience.

Pink describes 'our default setting to be autonomy'; it's an element of motivation in the twenty-first century.[9] He suggests people want autonomy over task, time, team and technique, the freedom to direct themselves. Empowerment meets this requirement.

'I'm encouraged to find better ways and feel
totally accountable for the change.'

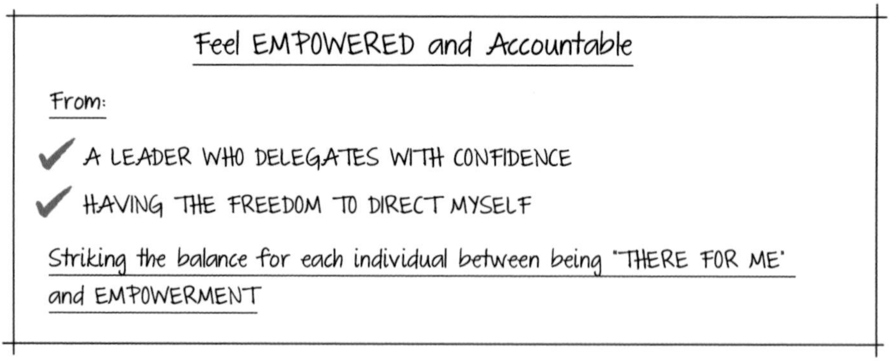

Feel EMPOWERED and Accountable

From:

✔ A LEADER WHO DELEGATES WITH CONFIDENCE
✔ HAVING THE FREEDOM TO DIRECT MYSELF

Striking the balance for each individual between being "THERE FOR ME" and EMPOWERMENT

Fig 7.9 Feel empowered and accountable

I feel he is contributing to my personal development

Not surprisingly this feeling derives from discussions with a leader who uses focusing on performance behaviours. People are grateful for constructive challenge, stretching assignments, coaching support, the encouragement to play to their strengths and honest feedback.

'I look forward to discussions with her;
she brings out the best in me.'

Prentice describes effective leadership as taking a personal interest in the long-term development of people:

> As long as you work for me I am going to see that you get every opportunity to use your last ounce of potential. Your growth and satisfaction are a part of my job. The faster you develop into a top contributor to this company, the better I shall like it. If you see a better way to do your job, do it that way; if something is holding you back, come and see me about it. If you are right, you will get all the help I can give you plus the recognition you deserve.[10]

Prentice also recognised that people are complex and that it's the leader's responsibility to tap into the specific needs of each.

I feel confident through working with him

This is an example of a positive impact on others coming from a variety of winning behaviours.

Firstly, from providing direction there's a confidence in the vision as 'the right thing to do'. It resonates with people.

> *'Relentless and consistent communication of priorities provides us with reassurance and confidence.'*

Secondly, from focusing on performance the dialogue builds belief in abilities and there's reassurance from reviewing actions that reinforces this.

> *'Having the freedom to act gives me confidence.'*

Finally, the biggest driver is the confidence the leader has in himself, which is transmitted to those around them.

> *'A sense of we can do it prevails and his confidence flows through to others.'*

The combination of a confident image with optimism inspires others.

Feel CONFIDENT

From:

✔ A VISION THAT RESONATES

✔ A BELIEF IN MY ABILITIES

✔ A LEADER WHO TRANSMITS A CONFIDENT IMAGE

Fig 7.10 Feel confident

I feel calm in potentially stressful situations

The leader's ability to lead themselves is the biggest contributor here. Controlling toxic emotions during difficult times is welcomed; it's as if the leader has the option to pass on the pressure he feels but chooses to provide a steadying influence in the belief that it will have a more positive impact on others and, ultimately, effect on performance outcomes. This choice does not go unnoticed.

> *'He brings a sense of calm to any conversation,*
> *which creates a positive feeling.'*

To a lesser degree this also comes through the engagement winning behaviours where a leader smoothes over tensions between individuals.

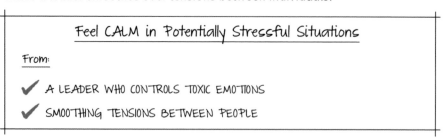

Feel CALM in Potentially Stressful Situations

From:

✔ A LEADER WHO CONTROLS TOXIC EMOTIONS

✔ SMOOTHING TENSIONS BETWEEN PEOPLE

Fig 7.11 Feel calm in potentially stressful situations

Let's end this chapter by looking at the impact of losing behaviours on others. The positive feelings we've already discussed are missing and the overriding impact is...

I feel unnecessary pressure to perform

Failing to avoid losing behaviours creates tension, anxiety and stress. People feel the brunt of the leader's feelings, impatience and frustration. False expectations and poor preparation impact as much on the reputations of the team as on the leader.

'Poor communication creates unnecessary pressure.'

There's an absence of any consideration for the feelings of others. Working with a boss who never listens is overbearing and demoralising.

'She needs to practise constructive challenge
rather than blunt questioning.'

Leaders' focus on themselves, their needs, their agenda and their feelings put unnecessary pressure on others to perform, particularly as they have the alternative of winning behaviours that have a very different impact on others.

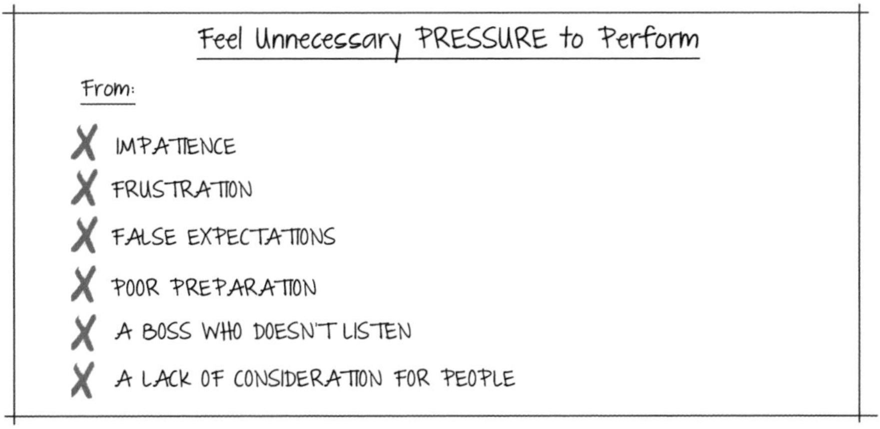

Feel Unnecessary PRESSURE to Perform

From:

X IMPATIENCE
X FRUSTRATION
X FALSE EXPECTATIONS
X POOR PREPARATION
X A BOSS WHO DOESN'T LISTEN
X A LACK OF CONSIDERATION FOR PEOPLE

Fig 7.12 Feel unnecessary pressure to perform

Alex read through Chris's latest feedback. He was preparing for Chris's performance review. Technically Chris is an outstanding finance director and great to be with socially. But for the third consecutive year his data was showing the strength of losing behaviours outweighing that of winning with the resulting impact on others. Chris was within two years of retirement and often talked about 'training someone up' to replace him but the impact Chris was having on others was a huge barrier to this. There was little or no chance of it happening. Alex read through the matrix that linked behaviour to impact on others (Fig 7.2). He imagined what it must feel like to miss the positive impact others in the organisation were getting. No one around Chris was performing to the best of their abilities in that environment. He knew it was his responsibility to share feedback, make it clear that Chris understood the implications of his behaviour, and offer support and praise where Alex had seen progress himself. Any failure to change after that would be Chris's own responsibility; Alex's conscience would be clear.

The impact winning (and losing) behaviours have on others has big implications for results. Alex therefore fulfilled the leadership responsibilities we explored in focus on performance.

In conclusion, one way of checking that we have all the bases covered here is to reflect on what you personally need to perform to the best of your ability. I'm suggesting it's a boss who provides clarity, is there for you, helps create a team spirit, empowers, motivates through rewards and high standards, contributes to personal development, ensures people remain calm in potentially stressful situations and instils confidence.

When a leader provides that environment I'm suggesting you will perform to the very best of your ability. It's interesting that a range of behaviours is required to create the impact that stimulates performance. Leaders need to be strong across all four winning behaviours.

Why not use the diagnostic to assess the impact your boss has on you and others; and from your knowledge of your relative strengths in the winning and losing behaviours the impact you feel you have on others?

Can you see the link from leadership behaviour to impact on others?

<u>How do you Rate this Individual's Impact on you and others?</u>

	DISAGREE STRONGLY		SOMEWHAT AGREE		AGREE STRONGLY	DON'T KNOW
PROVIDES THE CLARITY REQUIRED FOR PEOPLE TO DO THEIR BEST	☐	☐	☐	☐	☐	☐
CARES ABOUT PEOPLE AND CREATES OPEN AND TRUSTING RELATIONSHIPS	☐	☐	☐	☐	☐	☐
CREATES A SENSE OF TEAM SPIRIT	☐	☐	☐	☐	☐	☐
MOTIVATES AND INSPIRES OTHERS TO DO THEIR BEST WORK	☐	☐	☐	☐	☐	☐
EMPOWERS OTHERS AND MAKES THEM ACCOUNTABLE	☐	☐	☐	☐	☐	☐
CONTRIBUTES TO THE PERSONAL DEVELOPMENT OF OTHERS	☐	☐	☐	☐	☐	☐
PROVIDES CONFIDENCE TO OTHERS THROUGH WORKING WITH HIM/HER	☐	☐	☐	☐	☐	☐
CREATES APPROPRIATE CALMNESS IN POTENTIALLY STRESSFUL SITUATIONS	☐	☐	☐	☐	☐	☐
DOES NOT CREATE UNNECESSARY PRESSURE TO PERFORM	☐	☐	☐	☐	☐	☐

Part Three

Building Leadership Capability

CHAPTER 8

Getting Going

From my point of view this is the most important chapter and I am grateful to Simon Machin, because the majority of the content to this chapter is development material used successfully in Belron®. It is reproduced here with his kind permission.

As I mentioned at the very beginning I'm keen to demonstrate that there is a simple framework, winning behaviours, to describe the elements of leadership that make a difference, but what is more important is that you feel you want to try something different and be more effective. So now we'll look at ways to take what we have learned into a plan and do something about 'getting going'. We'll also look at how winning behaviours can help leaders in a new role, leadership transitions – a time when it is easy to lose focus on your own leadership.

Gary Lubner, the Belron® CEO throughout the research period, attended the development programmes where leaders were first introduced to their leadership feedback and data. He explained his approach to development:

> I am convinced that, whilst leadership is perhaps more art than science, we can provide some qualitative and quantitative tools to help understand leadership further. I believe learning is about three things: adding something to your mind, changing your mind and learning more about yourself. And a really important part of leadership, your task, is to drive yourself and other people in all three of these directions. Feedback provides you with a great opportunity to develop your leadership; please use it well.

Effective leadership development starts by first becoming aware of 'issues', often through feedback, sometimes through self reflection, and by then setting development goals. Only then can a focused development plan be constructed.

We'll use the following model, which is adapted from Machin, as a framework to track the development process.[1]

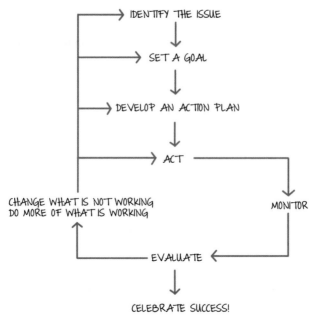

Fig 8.1 Achieving personal change

Identify the issue

The purpose of diagnostics like winning behaviours is to provide useful data, in the form of feedback, to surface issues that subsequently lead to development goals and the creation of plans.

Let's start by asking for feedback. The winning behaviours diagnostic is a simple feedback process: just fifty questions and seven opportunities to provide narrative evidence to support a rating. Appendix 20 summarises how you can create and use the approach we have shared in this book to gather feedback.

The responsibility for organising and collecting feedback is the line manager's. Ideally he would request this from people around the leader who are familiar with both their behaviours and their impact.

The style in which feedback is requested makes a big difference to the quality. It's important to explain that good feedback is a combination of what you see and the impact it has. Encourage people to schedule time in their diaries to focus on the request, give it the time it deserves; it won't take longer than an hour but encourage people to make time for this critical activity. Reinforce how important this is; and, of course, say thank you in advance.

In terms of output, you should be generating something like the summaries below but in your own format.

WINNING BEHAVIOURS SUMMARY

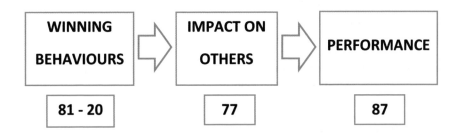

BEHAVIOURS

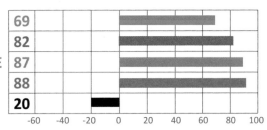

IMPACT ON OTHERS

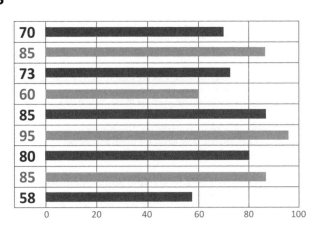

Fig 8.2 Winning behaviours summary

PROVIDING DIRECTION

Self
I rally the team around specific challenges
I can stand back and help people who are bogged down in detail
I constantly remind my team why customer retention is so important

Line Manager
He gains insights from many sources and shares to improve overall understanding
Regularly shares the company vision
His plans are always linked to company strategy

Direct Reports
Through constant reinforcement we are clear what we are doing and why
Short term actions are always linked to longer term goals
Comprehensive analysis keeps us ahead of our competitors

Peers
Sometimes comes across as wanting to demonstrate superior intellect
Could be more demonstrable about the things that matter
Spends too much time worrying about consumer expectations rather than doing something

Others
Seemingly endless curiosity, seeks insights from every part of the business
He has the whole team tuned into our philosophy on quality
He tends to keep the discussion focused on priorities rather than letting it drift.

Fig 8.3 Providing direction summary

What we can see are the key elements. At a high level they indicate which behaviours a leader is using, the impact those behaviours have on others and importantly their impact on performance. There's a score that gives an indication of relative strength and includes losing behaviours.

For the four winning behaviours, the losing behaviours and their impact on others, there's more detail. Providing direction is the example to the left. Here we can see the relative strength in the elements that comprise 'providing direction' and also from different perspectives, from self, line manager, direct reports, peers and in this example others who have experienced this individual's leadership, perhaps a project group he is involved with.

To support the ratings and help understand the feedback there's also narrative evidence.

It's comprehensive, which is good news, but it also requires time to reflect on the content, compare and contrast it with other feedback received and if appropriate discuss it with your line manager, a coach or a colleague whose opinion you value. It's a time to work through the emotions associated with learning something new to which you were previously blind.

We've discovered already that having people around the leader providing feedback in itself is not enough. A prerequisite is that the leader receiving feedback moves through denial and anger to acceptance. It requires that the feedback be received, digested, understood and put into context. Only then will self-awareness provide an accurate insight into the leadership issues that must be addressed.

Be patient; this stage may take some time. Look at a personal emotional release as a positive indication of progress.

Having received feedback and taken the time to reflect on or discuss it, you will be clear on what leadership issues others are seeing. For some it's the logic of the scores that brings the issues into focus; for others it's reading the comments people have kindly made. Don't forget that issues in our definition are as likely to be strengths you can make better use of, perhaps now you are aware, as they are to be areas for improvement.

The issue may be with one group rather than another. What am I doing on engagement with my team to get such a positive score? Why is it so low with peers? What can I deduce from that?

Is the issue to avoid losing behaviours or strengthen winning behaviours or both?

Does the narrative detail beneath an assessment of a winning behaviour explain which facet of this behaviour others are not seeing?

Can you see the link through behaviours to impact on others and on to results? What does this tell you?

Set a goal

Having established the issues, the next stage in our process is setting goals. However, this is not straightforward because there are a number of different aspects.

First are your own personal drivers, ambitions and aspirations – what you want now and what you want in the future. You will also need to consider the needs the organisation has, both now and in the future. You will want to think about your strengths as well as your weaknesses – great development is sometimes about how you can make more of your strengths, rather than plugging 'weakness gaps'. Another aspect may be how to get sufficient 'stretch' into your development.

Creating development goals that are genuinely engaging and exciting for you as a leader is critical to success. Often reframing goals, and describing them in a way that engages you, one that is concordant, will increase the likelihood of success.

For example, 'I need to provide more clarity for my team' may engage some but others may prefer, 'In the next year I'm going to experiment with different elements of providing direction so I can learn what works for me and my team'. Others may have an improvement in the rating as a goal. Because we are all different it's essential you select a goal that inspires you.

Leadership goals are set against two contexts: what's happening in the business and what the leader wants.

Let's start with the business context. The following questions will help shape this perspective:

- What are the responsibilities, accountabilities and deliverables of my current job?
- How will the requirements of my current job change over time, and in what way are they likely to be different from the current needs?
- What are my organisation's and my boss's approach and attitude towards leadership development?
- Are there opportunities for secondments or project work?
- In what ways do the organisation's strategy, vision and values align with my personal aspirations?
- What are the immediate action plans or operating plans for my part of the organisation, and how do they fit with my personal aspirations?
- Reflecting on both strategy and plans, what opportunities are there for the business and my personal aspirations to combine? What are the risks?

In summary, what do the answers to the above questions suggest in terms of broad leadership development? Where should the focus be?

Looking now at personal aspirations, it's essential that not only business needs are delivered but also that individuals feel both fulfilled and satisfied.

The following simple three-step process is designed to help you reflect on your personal aspirations.

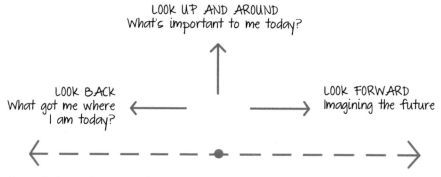

Fig 8.4 Understanding personal aspirations

The first step is to raise personal awareness of what made you the person you are today and how this might impact on you. One way to do this is a 'timeline exercise' where you plot a continuous line representing the positive and negative flow of your life to date.

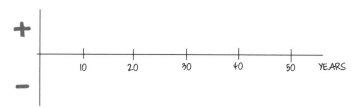

Fig 8.5 Timeline

Label some events, if it helps, and use the following questions to reflect:
- What does each part of the timeline mean to you?
- Which do you consider have been the happiest and most successful times?
- Which have caused you the most distress?
- What are the key events that were turning points and why?
- What key imperatives emerge?
- What patterns of behaviour show through? Are there other patterns (eg relationships)?

- What key messages can I take from the timeline?
- How do these messages impact on my current or future work?
- What are the implications for my development today?
- What energised and excited me in work, and what would I like to do more of?
- What sapped or reduced my energy in work, and would I prefer to do less of it?

The second step is to establish what is important to you today. The purpose of this step is to focus on your most significant values and the implication of these for you now. Rarely do we sit down and reflect on what is important to us. Understanding this is a key input to our development goals. One way to do this is to describe your personal values. Once you know what is important to you, you can stop spending so much time and energy on things that are less important and spend time on things that are more important to you.

Use the list of values below. Select the ten that are most important to you, feeling free to add, amend or create your own list.

Achievement	Freedom	Power and Authority
Advancement and Promotion	Friendships	Privacy
Adventure	Growth	Public Service
Affection (love and caring)	Having a Family	Purity
Arts	Helping other people	Quality of what I take
Challenging Problems	Helping Society	part in
Change and Variety	Honesty	Recognition (respect from
Close Relationships	Independence	others, status)
Community	Influencing others	Religious
Competence	Inner Harmony	Reputation
Competition	Integrity	Responsibility and
Conformity	Intellectual Status	Accountability
Cooperation	Involvement	Security
Creativity	Job Tranquillity	Self-respect
Decisiveness	Knowledge	Sophistication
Democracy	Leadership	Stability
Ecological Awareness	Loyalty	Status
Economic Security	Market Position	Supervising others
Effectiveness	Meaningful Work	Time Freedom
Efficiency	Merit	Travel
Ethical Practice	Money	Truth
Excellence	Nature	Wealth
Excitement	Being around people who	Where I work
Fame	are Open and Honest	Wisdom
Fast Living	Personal Development	Working under Pressure
Financial Gain	Physical Challenge	Working with others
	Pleasure	Working Alone

Fig 8.6 Personal values

- Which of these ten that you have selected are absolutely critical for you personally? For example, which are the top three?
- What do these mean for you?
- What would be the implication for you if these values were more prominent and practised in your work?
- If you were to focus on these what would be the implications for your development?

The final step is forward looking, imagining your future. To ensure your development goals are engaging and stretching, you have to dream. Counsellors who help people to stop smoking encourage them to see themselves as non-smokers, and those who wish to lose weight are told to picture themselves looking as they want to look. Imagining the future is a powerful input when creating development goals that inspire.

For example, imagine yourself ten to fifteen years in the future and living/working your ideal life. What kind of people would be around you? What does your environment look and feel like? What might you be doing during a typical day or week? Don't worry about how feasible this will be; just let the image develop.

Another alternative is to imagine yourself looking back over your life – what would be the things that please you, that raise a smile? What kind of legacy do you want to leave? How do you want to be remembered by others? What do you want to be remembered for?

Develop an action plan

This is the third stage in our process.

So now we know the leadership issues and we have looked at goals from both a personal and a business perspective. The next step is to write a plan. The act of committing to paper what you intend to do is very important. I've lost count of the number of people who, when receiving a rerun of their data and feedback, can't find their last set of feedback or their development plan (if it was written). They all have one thing in common: they do not make progress and invariably go backwards.

Before we commit to paper let's look at three principles to keep in mind when writing a plan.

Firstly, address your goals in a way that suits you best. There is so much written on self-improvement, personal development and changing your life. None of it matters if it doesn't work for you, so use a process that you are comfortable with.

Secondly, your change plan must fit with both your life and your work. If your plan isn't something that you can accommodate within your life, then it's unlikely that you will succeed.

Finally, your plan must tap into your preferred way of learning. Use your normal way of learning when taking on significant development. Doing otherwise can be frustrating and is unlikely to hold your attention. For example, don't try to learn on your own if you know that learning with others works better for you. There are two dimensions to the learning process: how people gather information and what they do with it. The following questions may provide insight into your preferred way of learning:

- Do you learn best from practically applying what you have learned immediately?
- Do you learn best from listening and observing, research and analysis, standing back and thinking things through?
- Do you learn best when being stretched intellectually?
- Do you learn best from having a go and getting involved?

The actual format of your plan is less important than the fact that you have written one. If you are looking for ideas, here are two different approaches.

One approach, for each leadership issue in your plan, is to list the actions you will take to build your proficiency and help you achieve your goal. Be clear on the deadlines for each activity, what support or help you require, and how you will know that progress has been made.

Overall Objective

INSPIRE OTHERS THROUGH A COMPELLING VISION OF THE FUTURE

Specific Actions

✔ DEVELOP MY 'VISION SPEECH' - IN LESS THAN ONE MINUTE BE ABLE TO EXPLAIN WHY IT IS AN IMPERATIVE

✔ IN DISCUSSION FOCUS ON WHY RATHER THAN WHAT

✔ AGREE WITH EACH OF MY TEAM WHERE THEY FIT IN AND THE SPECIFIC CONTRIBUTION THEY MAKE

✔ USE THE VISION TO HELP PRIORITISE

Support

✔ USE MY COACH AS A SOUNDING BOARD TO SHARE AND DISCUSS CRITICAL INCIDENTS - SCHEDULE A SESSION EVERY FIVE WEEKS

Evidence

✔ GATHER INFORMAL FEEDBACK FROM MY TEAM IN SIX MONTHS TO CHECK PROGRESS

I want people to be saying "I know why our work is so important and I know my contribution is both valued and appreciated"

Fig 8.7 Personal development plan

An alternative option is, having identified a behaviour for development, to list actions under the following headings

- What will I start doing to ensure development of this behaviour?
- What will I continue doing to ensure development of this behaviour?
- What will I stop doing to ensure development of this behaviour?

Key Objective

TO STRENGTHEN MY ENGAGEMENT BEHAVIOURS

Stop

✗ GETTING IMPATIENT IN MEETINGS

✗ IGNORING THE PERSONAL NEEDS OF MY TEAM

Continue

✓ HAVING CONVERSATIONS

✓ LISTENING TO PEOPLE

✓ GETTING TO KNOW MORE PEOPLE IN THE BUSINESS

Start

✓ THINKING ABOUT WHICH APPROACH TO USE IN ADVANCE

✓ BRING PERSONALITY AND EMOTIONS INTO PRESENTATIONS

✓ RELAXING!

Fig 8.8 Alternative personal development plan

I would encourage you to take challenge from a valued colleague on how likely your plan will achieve the goal you have set. Now is the time for a frank and honest discussion, not later.

Making and measuring progress

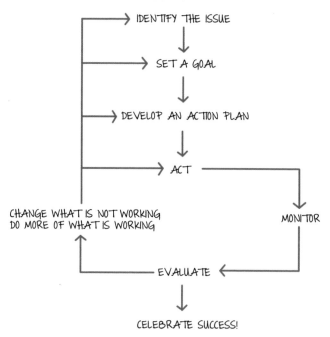

Fig 8.9 Achieving personal change

Having a plan, the next stage is to act on it. Elements of your plan may require you to do things differently. This is likely to feel awkward and uncomfortable, and there will be anxiety that it's not working simply because it doesn't feel natural. It's important to find a way to check, firstly, that your behaviour is perceived to have changed and, secondly, that the change is perceived positively.

Rick Lash called this ritualising behaviour, creating new habits.[2] 'It's about drill and practice, rewiring our neural pathways. These help fix new behaviours or attitudes, so they become more automatic or reflexive. The action must come first; the belief, so to speak, follows.'

When we looked at leading self we discussed how this is generally more difficult the more senior your position. A crucial part of this stage is knowing where you will get honest feedback. It's crucial because that's the encouragement leaders need to persevere with some new behaviours that, quite frankly, don't 'feel right' until they are embedded in their leadership psyche as a new way of doing things.

It's a fine line because you don't want to become known as a 'feedback junkie' either. It takes time for a change of behaviour to be perceived as a new recurring style by others, so be patient and have faith in your development plan. After six month's it's not unreasonable to gather informal feedback to confirm progress. In the meantime, discussing critical incidents such as one-to-ones or team meetings with your coach, a respected colleague or your boss can be helpful in spotting whether your winning behaviours are strengthening and your losing behaviours are receding. Simply use them as a sounding board and listen for the behaviours that underpin your stories. Some leaders use a coach to help prepare for key meetings with individuals or teams. They practise the behaviours they believe will be most impactful and then discuss what happened subsequently.

It's essential to keep focused on your behaviours and not the behaviours of your team.

Celebrate progress and, when evaluating, refine your plan to change what is not working and do more of what is. Constantly seek opportunities to build self-awareness.

One benefit of diagnostics such as winning behaviours is that they provide clear evidence of progress a year later.

Leadership transitions

Major job transitions can be a roller-coaster experience for leaders. A change of role brings pressures either from within the leader or just associated with the new job. Ironically, it's a common reason for a backward leadership step as those pressures encourage losing rather than winning behaviours in pursuit of results.

Let's look at the stages of transition and how winning behaviours can help.

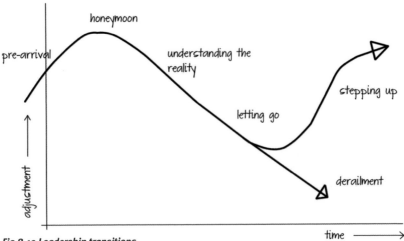

Fig 8.10 Leadership transitions

The transition typically goes through several steps: pre-arrival, honeymoon, understanding the reality, letting go and stepping up.

With pre-arrival comes relief, anticipation and apprehension as the leader is too busy getting out of the old role to plan getting into a new one.

During the honeymoon period there's excitement and self-affirmation. It's a time when the leader is given slack because they are not expected to know. But there's possibly a lack of realism associated with this time, ignoring negative evidence and others colluding rather than genuinely sharing.

Pressures build as the leader starts to understand the reality; they become aware of unexpected truths and there's a shift suddenly to a position where they are expected to know, which often comes unsignalled. Potentially, lack of cultural alignment (not understanding the behavioural norms) compounded by lack of clarity on what is actually expected leaves the leader unclear, confused and perhaps anxious.

During the letting go phase, there's a tendency to doubt confidence, and a need to let go of unrealistic expectations and stop clinging to things that worked in the past. In accepting the new reality and responsibilities may come anger, depression and derailment.

The will to win kicks in with stepping up. The leader constructs a new professional identity, and priorities get clear as the leader accepts the upsides and downsides of the new role. With that they start to succeed.

If that's the roller-coaster of a promotion or new challenge, let's look at how the winning behaviours of providing direction, engagement, focus on performance and leading self can help when planning development to support a successful transition.

Such a plan is based around understanding the business, establishing priorities, early wins and making the right impact. Below I've summarised the tasks a leader needs to cover in the first nine months.

Make learning a top priority
- Appreciate your strengths that got you where you are, but also be honest about blind spots and development needs. Make plans to cover them.
- Create a learning agenda for yourself and work on it.
- Spend time walking around, talking with people and asking questions. Take time to watch, listen and experience.
- Frankly assess the situation you are in so your plans can reflect reality.
- Keep reflecting on what you have learnt.

Get your agenda right

- Develop your decisions, goals and plans based on what you have learnt.
- Focus on what is important, both now and longer term.

Make a positive impact early on

- Move decisively for quick wins and improvements (ensure these are seen as important to others, achievable given your resources and a chance to model desired behavioural norms).
- When practical and wise, start communicating your longer-term agenda.
- Manage your image and attend to feedback.
- Demonstrate how you make decisions, and your personal values, energy and beliefs.

Build your team

- Listen and learn (to the team and your peers). Learn about the team (their strengths and weaknesses), and what motivates individuals.
- Critically examine your team both individually and collectively.
- Evaluate the potential and any need for change.

Build partnerships

- Involve key stakeholders in your thinking and planning, and be certain to understand their needs.
- Understand the political landscape. How are things done around here?
- Let your team and their teams know your agenda (and ask for their reactions and input).
- Build personal credibility.
- Prepare carefully for your meetings and presentations, think about the audience and ensure your priorities are clear.
- Maximise team success and work through others.

Align with your new boss

- Early on, specifically discuss expectations and how success will be measured.
- Discuss your agenda and priorities, and ask the boss for input.
- Agree on available resource your line manager will offer to support your agenda.
- Learn your boss's preferred style and methods of communication.

Reflect and build relationships

- Which relationships are strong and positive, and how can you build on these?
- Which relationships are you more concerned about, and how can you address these?

Authenticate your leadership

- Develop a picture of how you want to lead in your new role.
- Where are you now? How can you close the gaps?

Think about yourself

- Sustain your personal drive and manage your own frustration.
- Get feedback (starting with the recruitment process) and adjust your behaviour accordingly.
- Make time for yourself and your family. How is this new role impacting on your wider system?

Focus on delivery

- Demonstrate progress on the commitments you have made; these are your responsibility.
- Seek opportunities to reinforce that the priorities are right, or refine.
- Encourage people to focus on the things that will actually make a difference.

There are also some transition risks to avoid, not surprisingly associated with the losing behaviours.

Knowing it all

- Overconfidence, believing you know best before you actually do.
- Using old solutions, or previous experience to solve new problems.
- Failing to ask questions, and not listening carefully to what's really going on.
- Lack of awareness in frequently referring to your old organisation and how they did things.

Doing it all

- Trying to do too much, too soon.
- Failing to manage expectations appropriately.
- Becoming isolated, and working behind closed doors.
- Not effectively letting go of the former job's responsibilities (common with an internal promotion).

Assuming it all

- Failing to check for understanding and buy-in, thereby obtaining compliance rather than commitment.
- Not rigorously evaluating your people, perhaps assuming they are competent, correctly placed, and motivated by the right things.
- Believing people will support and respect you because you are the boss.
- Assuming your strengths in your former job will translate directly to your new one.

Whilst these are suggestions for a transition plan, some may be appropriate in light of feedback you have received in your existing role. Do any strike a chord with you?

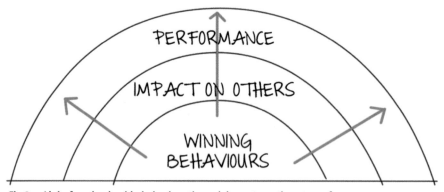

Fig 8.11 Links from leadership behaviour through impact on others to performance

Throughout the book the theme has been that behaviours through an impact on others generate a positive organisation outcome. It may look tempting to focus on the impact you are having on others as the main aspect of your development plan, but from experience the root cause, the underlying behaviour, is more likely to be a more successful route. In Chapter 7 we explored the links between winning behaviours and their impact on others. If you want a reminder have a look at Fig 7.2.

When putting together a development plan, don't forget what Kim discovered in Chapter 4: activities and behaviours are completely different. The activity of coaching can be done using any combination of winning and losing behaviours. Likewise, holding a meeting and sharing a vision are activities that can be done using an array of behaviours. It's the behaviours your plan should focus on.

Finally, I have a personal reflection on my own feedback. I had a particularly large gap between what my team wanted in terms of reward and what I was delivering.

They were kind enough to give me the following examples to help me understand.

'In our one-to-ones you are always smiling and good-humoured. I'm never sure if you give me all the feedback. Sometimes it would be good to hear that things are just OK and discuss what I could have done different.'

'You benchmarked my pay last year.' 'I know,' was my response, 'and I amended your pay.' 'I appreciate that but I still don't quite see how the benchmark process worked.'

'Other members of the team present to the Main Board but I don't get the chance. My work isn't appreciated as much as theirs and I don't see why.'

Feedback is the perception of others but to them it's a reality and they feel the impact. In the above examples it was a reality to which I was completely blind until I was fortunate enough to get the feedback. When I initially received the examples, they didn't appear to be a big issue to me but that's not the point. The impact they had on others and the gap they perceived from me on rewards is the reality ... not my own paradigm of what I thought I was doing through 'rose tinted glasses'. The lesson for me was that if people are good enough to provide feedback, take it at face value, see it from their perspective and commit to doing something about it.

From my experience I can also share what has worked for others. There are some recurring themes:

- Commit to a plan, and write it down.
- Involve others.
- Improve self-awareness.
- Be clear about exactly what you are trying to do and the impact it will have.
- Link development to either a business need or a personal aspiration.
- See leadership as the job and not an extra task.

So, in summary, the important thing is to try something different, just 'get going'. The impact on others and your organisation will follow.

CHAPTER 9
Organisational Support

From an organisational perspective Belron® put leadership behaviours at the centre of its development agenda. Recruitment, training, coaching and performance management were the key initiatives behind the dramatic improvement in leadership calibre that supported the organisation's strategy of profitable growth.

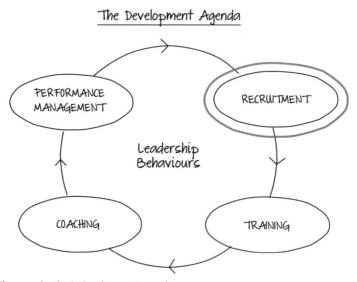

Fig 9.1 The organisation's development agenda

Recruitment

Belron® chose to start with recruitment. It's a rapidly growing organisation so we consciously decided to focus on bringing the 'right' leaders into the business.

When Belron® recruits, whilst it does take skills, knowledge and experience into account, it largely relies on the recruitment agency or head hunter to assess CVs for this. Belron® then runs assessment centres itself, with role plays and exercises that allow potential candidates the opportunity to demonstrate their relative strengths in the behaviours Belron® seeks from leaders. Over time a rigour has developed in these assessment centres that has shifted from 'first past the post' or select 'the best on the day' to an assessment of whether a level of competency has been demonstrated. It is not unusual to need more than one assessment centre and frequently we find ourselves at an airport taking a call from a colleague and discussing how things have gone. Even if no one is found to be suitable after a particular assessment centre, the reaction is invariably: 'Sounds like a good day's work then.'

Whilst it may not feel like that at the time for the one anticipating the long trip home, it's true. The behaviours we see in an assessment centre are exactly those we will see from that candidate in the job, which is why Belron® perseveres with the process.

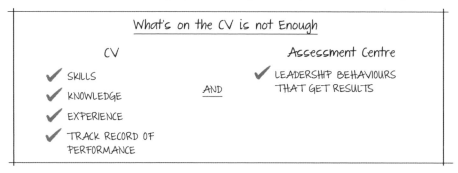

Fig 9.2 What's on the CV is not enough

When I reflect, in the early days of assessment centres we lacked the discipline to believe the evidence of behaviour we gathered. There's always the temptation to recruit to fill the gap, because surely having someone in place is better than having no one? We eventually learnt that's simply not the case. It's likely, indeed very likely if you've already seen the evidence, that they will have a negative impact on those around them just by being there.

Recruiting in haste and ignoring the behavioural evidence gathered condemns the organisation to an underperforming executive, undermines the culture you are seeking and, as importantly, is not a fair deal for the one appointed. You also fail to meet the organisation's obligations to the people who will work for the new leader. They are going to fail and you know it already! Six months to a year later you'll gather the feedback and find the assessment centre was accurate. That was our experience so eventually we became clear on the hurdle to be jumped and refused to move from that standard no matter how much we all felt the imperative to just 'fill the gap'.

Sometimes the employment agency would say the references are good – 'Just look at what they have done in their last job' – or state that they were not like that in the interview. It's true: being successful in the interview was not an indicator of being successful at the assessment centre or in the job itself. Indeed, research indicates that conducting an interview and taking references will give you a 20 per cent chance the successful candidate will flourish in the role. Only by including a structured interview around competencies, psychometrics and behaviour based role-plays will you increase the chances of success to 70 per cent.[1]

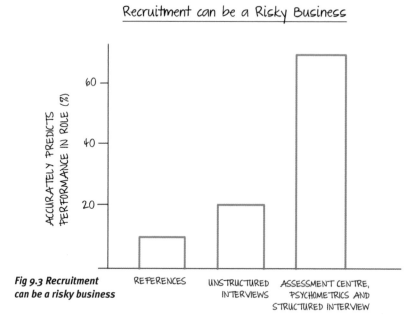

Fig 9.3 Recruitment can be a risky business

It was a recurring theme to the way Belron® recruited that the structured interview was not a good predictor of who would succeed in the assessment centre or in the role. Sometimes it was, sometimes it wasn't; too big a risk in my opinion. Yet for many organisations that's still the way they select.

Recruiting general managers is the extreme example of the importance of leadership behaviour to Belron®. The job role would state that the responsibility of a general manager is to lead a team of outstanding functional heads. Invariably we would seek someone who had done the job elsewhere, and enjoyed it so much they wanted to do it again in Belron®. When asked by the head hunter whether marketing expertise, key account management or operational experience were required, our response was: 'No, certainly not. We have functional experts in all those areas. The job of the successful candidate is to lead them.'

I read a personal development plan once that had as its overriding goal: 'I must remember that my team know how to do the task far better than I do. My job is to lead them.' How true that is. Of all the roles in an organisation, I'm sure that applies most to a general manager, but how many follow that sound advice?

Internal candidates went through the same process as external candidates. Belron® had no preference for one over the other; it was simply looking for the best against the standard. If, however, an internal and an external candidate were both of the standard required, Belron® would select the internal candidate simply because the assessment centre observations (just one day) were supported by a wealth of behaviour data over a number of years.

Whilst it's a lengthy and time-consuming process, Belron® learnt that the costs of getting it wrong make it an investment well worth while. The result invariably was that Belron® was confident it had the right person and, just as importantly, the successful candidate having cleared all the hoops was very confident they were entering a role that suited them and in which they would perform.

The responsibility for making the appointment was the local line manager's. The role of the centre was to provide support and ensure the process described was followed. Belron® built a pool of people trained in what Rob Ashmore describes as ORCEF: observation, recording, classification, evaluation and feedback.[2] The quality of their work ensured Belron® made the right appointments, candidates gained the insights they needed on their behaviour and, specifically for the successful candidate, the first input to their personal development plan.

Buckingham and Coffman make a number of suggestions on how to make best use of a structured interview when looking for the right behaviours, which Belron® applied.[3] For example, listening for responses that imply a behaviour is in constant use. 'Only yesterday I …' and 'Last week I …' rather than an answer that could conceivably have been from someone else or from a book. The answers to open questions are likely to be great indicators, even if they're not what you want to hear.

I'm not suggesting that skills knowledge and experience are not important; simply that they are much easier to check than the things that make a real difference, the soft skills or leadership behaviours. These are more difficult to tease out but vital if you wish to create a high performance culture. That's where the winning behaviours lie and subsequently that's where I chose to focus my research.

Ali was settled in his old job but was mildly curious when a head hunter approached with a new opportunity. It had been an odd process, although the head hunter had briefed him about the assessment day. Whilst he had been anxious because it was such an unusual experience and it was certainly exhausting because it had been so comprehensive, it had left Ali feeling that his prospective employer knew him inside out and that if he was right for the job he'd certainly get it. Despite the intensity of the assessment he'd actually met all the senior team during the day. He wondered what kind of company made such a commitment to the simple task of recruiting a financial director, reflecting however, that it had definitely built his commitment.

Ali was successful. He'd been looking forward to his first day at work – there was so much that needed to be done – but he was in for another surprise. Alex, his new boss, was looking for no more from their first one-to-one than completing an induction plan for the first four weeks. Alex made it clear to Ali that he expected nothing from him until he'd had the chance to move around the business, meet people and listen to what they had to say and how they felt. 'It's the best chance you'll get to do that openly,' he joked. At the end of the month they'd meet again to hear what Ali had observed and learnt, and for Alex to share with Ali the feedback from the assessment centre.

'Curiouser and curiouser,' thought Ali.

Recruitment is quite simply about getting the best person into the role, a combination of skills, experience and the leadership behaviours to get results. When we looked at role transitions in Chapter 8, we discovered the importance of a thorough induction period to an executive's subsequent success in a new role.

Training
Belron® developed training material to encourage understanding of leadership behaviours and in some cases deliver the first set of feedback. For the executive population the focus is on behavioural change rather than on knowledge acquisition.

Belron® created a range of modules to encourage understanding of the competencies summarised in Appendix 14. The programmes were delivered in-house and were seen as an opportunity also to bring leaders from across Belron® together. Where appropriate the senior team were involved to share their perspectives on the behaviours and their personal experience of the change journey. The CEO always attended when new Belron® leaders received their first set of leadership data. Gary shared his own feedback and his personal view on why leadership is important. This served to demonstrate that leadership genuinely is a Belron® priority.

The programmes were successful in the sense that feedback (about the programmes) was good; they raised awareness about the importance of leadership and, because the material addressed a range of learning preferences, understanding improved. However, Belron® did not see the improvement in

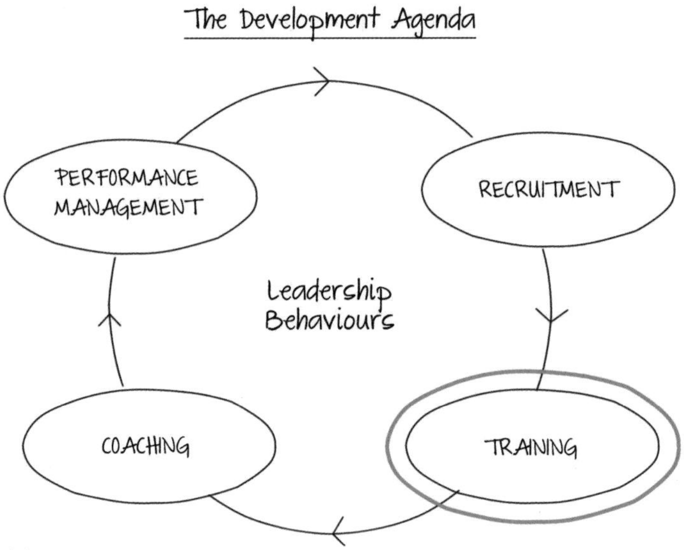

The Development Agenda

Fig 9.4 Training

leadership calibre it was seeking. That came subsequently through a combination of coaching and performance management.

Having said that, there's no doubt that having something highly visible supported by key players, which reinforces the organisation's culture in the way it is delivered, put leadership firmly on the Belron® map. It certainly raised the profile of leadership and an appreciation for the stakes involved to improve. Of all the items on the development agenda it was, however, the biggest investment of time and resource.

On reflection, some programmes were easier to design than others. Not surprisingly, those were the ones that focused less on leadership behaviour than on management skills. This meant that Belron® got to grips with the behaviours associated with achieving performance through others in the last two modules we designed and delivered. It is possibly another reason we didn't see the early improvement in leadership calibre anticipated.

Coaching

The most effective support to improve personal leadership was coaching. Coaching was offered rather than thrust on individuals. The request came usually in response to a poor set of feedback. Appendix 11 shows the impact this had. Where leaders are blind to the behaviours they use and the impact they have, even when it is clear as day to everyone else (Appendix 9) a coach is essential. They provide the

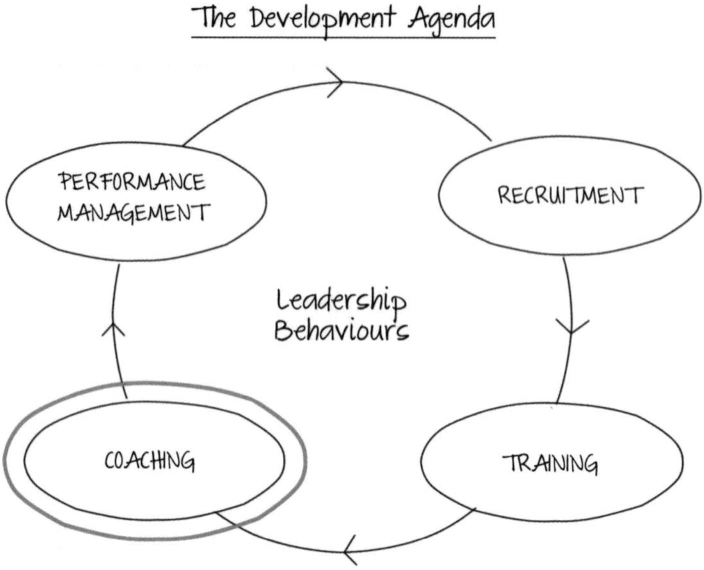

The Development Agenda

Fig 9.5 Coaching

technical skills, emotional intelligence and patience to build awareness and work through the feelings associated with gaining that knowledge.

Alternatively, requests came from executives wanting to strengthen their behaviours to prepare themselves for a bigger or different role.

Finally a coach usually helped with an executive new to the business; sometimes a person from the central leadership team who helped with the recruitment and assessment.

Best practice is to contract on deliverables with a coach and agree this with the line manager to gain commitment from them also to the process.

Whether the coach was internal or external, the measure of success was common. As leaders we were all measured in the same way, which ensured a real focus to that coaching relationship. Coaches are free to use whatever techniques they feel are appropriate but the impact will be judged objectively against the Belron® leadership KPI.

Organisationally, coaching workshops were run to build capability and offer more support specifically from line managers. The technical skills of internal coaches were developed and coaching supervision was encouraged.

A questionnaire was developed by Simon Machin to assess the coach as a person, the relationship with the coach, the coaching process, general feedback on what helped and didn't and of course how successful the coaching programme had been (in meeting specified goals and objectives).[4] This was used to develop our internal coaching capability.

Performance management

Fig 9.6 Performance management

Scores, scores, scores! That was the breakthrough for Belron® in managing the performance of its executives. Three hundred and sixty degree feedback had been a feature since the mid nineties but the advent of a score for leadership gave it a life of its own to complement the quality of the narrative comments.

Leadership feedback and scores are always positioned as an aid to development. For example, the first set of data leaders receive is likely to be poor; that's what our research in Appendix 3 showed. The Belron® approach was: 'That's fine, you don't know what you don't know. But now you do and you also appreciate why leadership is so important to Belron®. We will offer you whatever support you require and we expect to see an improvement when we rerun in a year's time.' I don't believe that's an unreasonable request.

There are a number of things that make a difference in terms of success or failure. Firstly, there's a score, a way to measure progress. Secondly, and for some leaders the more compelling reason to change, there's narrative feedback. Belron® invested time in feedback workshops, making it clear what good and bad feedback looked like and encouraging comments. Finally, there's the knowledge that in a year's time there will be a rerun.

Combine this with the fact that your own leadership 'score' contributes to the local composite (and the corporate measure), the offer of support to improve, the coaching, and the focus on leadership generated momentum.

Appendices 2 and 15 demonstrate how Belron® measured leadership. Whilst there was a commitment to maintain anonymity, other than with a leader's line manager, every executive knew exactly where they stood compared to their peers. We prepared composites for functional forums, anything to maintain a healthy competition around improvement.

I recall a leader telling me about a great programme they had been on – how much they had learnt about leadership and themselves, and how they had received some insightful feedback – only for that data to gather dust in a drawer because there was no follow-up. That's one of the things that makes Belron® special: leadership does matter and that's why there is an annual 'check-up'.

It does take time for an individual to give quality feedback and rate a Belron® executive but it's an investment that generates comments and scores to track progress and encourage further development. The performance management process was designed to provide executives with the best possible feedback.

From an organisation perspective, recruitment through assessment for key behaviours in addition to skills and experience supported by training, coaching and performance management processes that focus on the same behaviours were the company agenda that underpinned the transformation in leadership calibre we see in Appendix 4, and that drove the business results summarised in Appendix 19.

Are the winning behaviours future-proof?

Many organisations are tempted to change their competencies; indeed, do so frequently. Unless there is concrete evidence that your competencies do not encourage performance, I would resist the temptation.

I believe that it is not the competencies that have made such a big difference in Belron® but what Belron® has done with them through recruitment, training, coaching and performance measurement. The competency frameworks of other organisations are very similar. If you look through the summary in Appendix 14 I don't think you'll find anything 'special'. Experience over the last ten years has demonstrated that this enthusiasm for leadership development is based on a fundamental belief that the behaviours associated with the competencies, EI (emotional intelligence) drivers and appropriate leadership styles have genuinely delivered results in the past.

Belron® regularly reviews its strategy. In 2010, it did so again. There were a number of common themes that emerged from the strategic initiatives planned for the next five years, partly in response to an external analysis of future trends. I've focused below solely on the leadership behaviours that are required to deliver the Belron® strategy over that period. My instinct is that they will be familiar to most organisations:

- adopting greater pace and urgency to deliver strategy through others;
- using the phrase 'step change' consistently;
- communicating why something is a priority, getting it on the agenda and keeping focused until delivery; and
- building relationships but with a clear purpose or outcome in mind.

A sense of imperative runs through these and there's the possible temptation to tell or show 'the way' as the quickest route. From what we have discovered, however, large, global (dispersed) and fast-growing organisations are better served by leaders who provide direction, engage with their people, focus on performance and lead themselves. Requiring the leader to be present is actually a constraint to growth. Success does, however, rely on followers being comfortable with responsibility and accountability.

Only winning behaviours will consistently get the key messages through to those in a position to deliver at the pace and to the standard required. Losing behaviours are a constraint to delivering strategy in fast-growing businesses. Ironically it's the very pressure to deliver more quickly and remotely that makes winning behaviours the only way to lead.

Organisational leadership learnings

Let's summarise by capturing some of my organisational learnings.

Measurement is important to drive a change in leadership behaviour. It was consistent with the culture of Belron® and it helped individuals understand themselves. I have seldom met executives with a low achievement drive and the concept of a score with a bit of healthy competition appeals to most. It enables individuals to set goals and to measure progress against these. Finally it demonstrates progress to line managers on what is an important organisational KPI. When an executive engages a coach it gives them a measureable outcome to focus on together.

The low hanging fruit, and by that I mean putting together and delivering a training programme to support the sharing of a leader's first set of feedback and data, did not have the biggest impact. The experience of Belron® was that personal coaching made the biggest difference and particularly for those who started with what I'll refer to as the 'losing behaviours'. In the absence of follow-up coaching or support the rerun of leadership data was at best the same.

Having leadership KPIs as part of the annual budgeting and operating plan process ensured traction. Having thirty-three general managers appreciate that it was a Belron®-wide KPI, measured consistently, gave leadership the same focus as profitable growth, customer service and staff satisfaction. Each business would update on progress in the last year, and set a target for the coming year with the plans to ensure further progress.

Personal development is the individual's responsibility, but it's the responsibility of the organisation to explain why it is so important and offer whatever support is required. Ultimately, though, the executive rather than Belron® is responsible for personal development as a leader.

Having the right competency framework is not the biggest issue; it's what you do with it. Throughout the period covered, the Belron® competencies remained unchanged. I'm convinced that most organisations have a set of competencies that are 90 per cent right. Nudging that up is not the problem companies face. It's more to do with focusing on leadership behaviours relentlessly through recruitment, training, performance management and coaching.

Role-modelling behaviour extended to doing it in practice. Appendix 8 shows the transformation in the leadership calibre of firstly the senior team and secondly the general managers. It's interesting that as groups their first sets of data are no different from those of leaders in general.

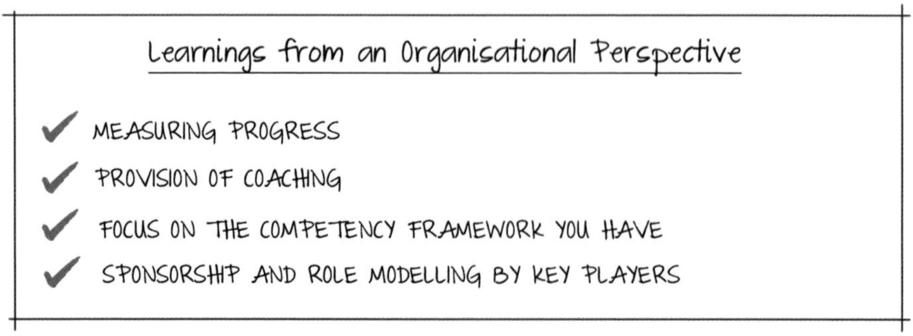

Learnings from an Organisational Perspective

✔ MEASURING PROGRESS

✔ PROVISION OF COACHING

✔ FOCUS ON THE COMPETENCY FRAMEWORK YOU HAVE

✔ SPONSORSHIP AND ROLE MODELLING BY KEY PLAYERS

Fig 9.7 Learnings from an organisational perspective

Absence of an organisational approach that supports personal leadership development is not an excuse for a leader to do nothing. There is, however, no doubt that a combination of an organisation and individual motivated to develop is indeed compelling.

Part Four

Conclusions

CHAPTER 10

Pulling It All Together

In Chapter 1 I set myself the personal challenge that 'by the end of the book you will understand the elements of leadership behaviour better and feel encouraged to do something different'. I also asked you to reflect on the behaviours you had seen from both good and bad bosses together with the impact those behaviours had on others.

I'll let you be the judge of how well I've met that challenge. Do you think I have captured your views on what differentiates a good boss from a bad one? Throughout the book the focus has been on how leadership behaviours impact on others to generate an outcome for the organisation. In other words, we've concentrated on leadership that drives results rather than leadership for its own sake as something of value intrinsically.

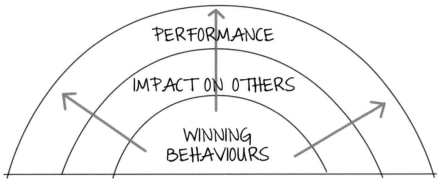

Fig 10.1 Leadership that drives results

The winning behaviours are a simple framework that embodies traditional leadership competencies, emotional intelligence competencies and the positive aspect of Hay Group's resonant styles into four key elements. Appendices 14 and 17 explain how the winning behaviours embrace all those aspects of leadership.

Rick Lash sums it up as people who 'possess aptitudes such as personal honesty and integrity, consensus building, a keen interest in the long term development of others, a capacity to manage their emotions and an ability to communicate a compelling vision to others'.[1]

In pulling it all together and by way of summary I'd like to offer three different perspectives on winning behaviours.

The first is on the receiving end of leadership. Buckingham and Coffman state that measuring the strength of a workplace can be simplified to twelve questions.[2] This conclusion was based on interviewing more than a million people using Gallup. Winning behaviours, not surprisingly, fit their conclusion:

1. Do I know what is expected of me at work?
2. Do I have the materials and tools to do my job right?
3. At work, do I have the opportunity to do what I do best every day?
4. In the last seven days, have I received recognition or praise for good work?
5. **Does my supervisor, or someone at work, seem to care about me as a person?**
6. Is there somebody at work who encourages my development?
7. **At work, do my opinions seem to count?**
8. Does the mission/purpose of my company make me feel like my work is important?
9. **Are my co-workers committed to doing quality work?**
10. **Do I have a best friend at work?**
11. In the last six months, have I talked with someone about my progress?
12. In the last year, have I had opportunities at work to learn and grow?

Belron® included those questions, as a minimum, in all employee engagement surveys.

The second is a reflection on how leaders are selected for promotion. Beeson's article 'Why You Didn't Get That Promotion' summarises the key factors in executive career advancement as follows:[3]

Core selection factors
- Setting direction and thinking strategically, spotting marketplace trends and developing a winning strategy that differentiates the company.
- Building and upgrading a strong executive team, and having a nose for talent.
- Establishing an adequate level of team cohesion.
- Managing implementation without getting involved at too low a level of detail.
- Defining a set of roles, processes and measures to ensure that things get done reliably.
- Building the capacity for innovation and change. Having the courage, tolerance for risk and change management skills to bring new ideas to fruition.
- Getting things done across internal boundaries, influencing and demonstrating political 'savvy'.
- Growing and developing as an executive, soliciting and responding to feedback, and adjusting leadership style in the light of experience.

These are also a very good fit with our winning behaviours.

And perhaps not surprisingly the de-selection factors sit nicely with our losing behaviours:

De-selection factors
- Having weak interpersonal skills.
- Treating others with insensitivity or abrasiveness.
- Putting self-interest above company good.
- Holding a narrow parochial perspective on the business and the organisation.

The third is another look at the ICE model I introduced in Chapter 3, which tracks the organisational critical activities of gathering ideas, through to funnelling and investing in a few before acting on the most promising.[4]

Let's consider where winning behaviours fit in:

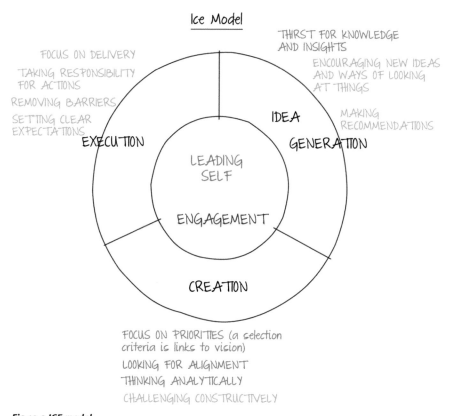

Fig 10.2 ICE model

The behaviours associated with engagement and the ability to lead self are key throughout all three stages. There would be either no dialogue or a one-sided discussion without them. I consider these behaviours the oil that lubricates the process.

In the idea generation phase, the behaviours of showing a thirst for knowledge and insights, encouraging new ideas and ways of looking at things, and making recommendations play a big part.

At the end of the creation stage there's a clear sense of direction as a result of a focus on priorities, seeking alignment, thinking analytically and providing constructive challenge.

Execution comes from a focus on delivery, taking responsibility for actions, removing barriers and setting clear expectations.

Pulling it all together, I'd like to summarise what we've shared as follows:

Through the behaviours associated with providing direction people appreciate clarity on priorities and encouragement to take action. It leaves them feeling reassured and confident. Through the engagement behaviours there's a sense that the leader is there 100 per cent for them and the open dialogue builds trust, respect and a sense of team spirit. There's engagement on two levels, with the individual and a group or team. The behaviours associated with focus on performance provide freedom to act with accountability and to challenge constructively. A combination of support and praise leaves people feeling valued and confident in their abilities. There's an energy that comes from high standards. In leading self, the ability to manage emotions, either as a calming influence in stressful times or in terms of energising people to 'go for it', whilst showing optimism inspires those around the leader. It instils confidence in others.

The Winning Behaviours

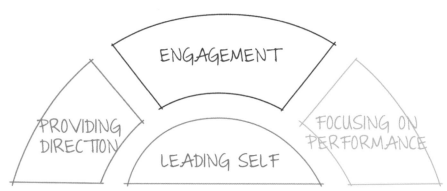

Fig 10.3 Winning behaviours

These are the winning behaviours.

Returning again to the first chapter, there's a winning mindset that leadership is your job and not part of your job. In all roles the list of things to do is seemingly endless, but winners see leadership as a way to get things done quicker, better and through others. Losers will get results but at a cost. The impact on others will be corrosive and what is achieved through telling, showing or doing will be constrained by their own standards, ability and creativity.

From a personal leadership point of view as well as an organisational perspective, winning behaviours are the key to delivering outstanding results. Good luck with your leadership development.

Appendices

Appendix 1

Hay Group methodology and definitions

Belron® research focused on two types of feedback, one of which was a Hay Group tool that traces leadership styles through to the climate those styles create specifically for direct reports to the leader. Hay Group research indicates that the styles used by a leader are responsible for 70 per cent of the climate experienced by direct reports. And through a high performance climate leadership can explain up to 30 per cent of the variance in performance through discretionary effort. The Hay Group four circle model below describes this. There are two other elements: the leader's personal characteristics and the role they are in. Both play a part in helping understand how effective a leader can be. We explored this when we looked at goal setting in Chapter 8. However, Belron® focused on the styles and climate data gathered, those closest to the impact on performance.

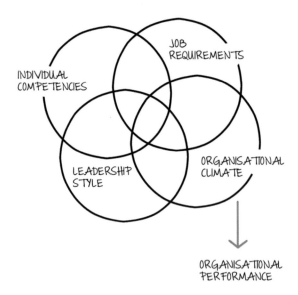

The attraction to Belron® was that there is an output to leadership and in climate a way of assessing how effective a leader is in getting results through their direct reports. It was originally used to support development on two competencies of Belron®, leading others and developing talent.

Belron® assessed the styles used by leaders and the climate created by them from 2002 to 2010, the majority of the period researched. Six hundred sets of styles and climate data were analysed as part of the research.

The definitions of leadership styles and dimensions of organisational climate

Goleman defines the Hay Group leadership styles as follows:[1]

Coercive: Demands immediate compliance.
Authoritative: Mobilises people toward a vision.
Affiliative: Creates harmony and builds emotional bonds.
Democratic: Forges consensus through participation.
Pacesetting: Sets high standards for performance.
Coaching: Develops people for the future.

To picture the behaviours associated with those styles imagine a leader who thinks only in the way described in the definition. That will give you a good feel. Leaders use anything from none to all of these styles to create a positive climate for their direct reports. Any style that is perceived as recurring or consistent is described as dominant, seen by others as used regularly to get results.

And the definitions of the Hay Group organisational climate dimensions are:[2]

Flexibility: There are no unnecessary rules, procedures, policies or practices. New ideas are easily accepted.
Responsibility: Employees are given authority to accomplish tasks without having to constantly check for approval.
Standards: Challenging but attainable goals are set for the organisation and its employees.
Reward: Employees are recognised and rewarded for good performance.
Clarity: Everyone within the organisation knows what is expected of him or her.
Team commitment: People are proud to belong to the organisation.

For both the styles and climate it is the Hay Group definition that is critical and not, for example, a personal view on what authoritative or coercive means.

Appendix 2
Measuring leadership capability through climate created

It's climate, and specifically one where each direct report gets an actual climate close to that which they personally seek on each dimension (the ideal), that encourages performance through direct reports. A gap of 20 per cent or more on any dimension impacts performance; three in the Hay Group Organisational Climate Survey example overleaf.

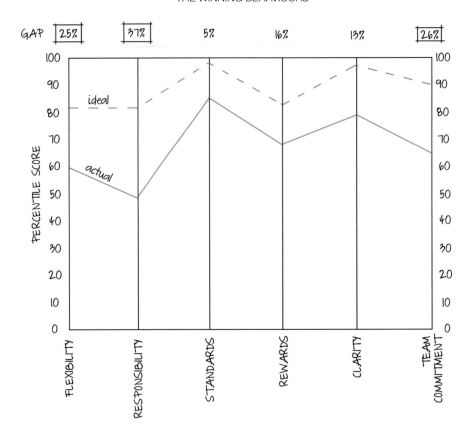

Belron® used climate (because it is closer to results than the styles used) as a measure of leadership calibre. Three dimensions of climate are proven to have a greater impact on performance, clarity, standards and team commitment, so these were given more weight in the way Belron® assesses leadership.

It's a rigorous measure of leadership. Firstly there are far more ways to be de-motivating than to be high performance. Secondly because a gap of 20 percentage points between what direct reports expect (their ideal) on a dimension of climate and what they get (the actual) was defined as a gap, whereas 19 is not a gap. That is consistent with Hay Group research. The example climate graph in this appendix would be analysed as neutral, one significant gap on the three dimensions having the biggest impact and two on the others.

The neutral climates created by leaders are tolerable to direct reports but are not tapping into their intrinsic motivation. In all other categories people are impacted by the leader's behaviour, either positively or negatively.

The executive population were plotted on this matrix. Below is the summary

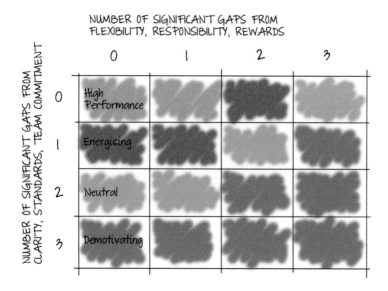

for executives in post at December 2009. For some it was their first set of data and, of course, 'you don't know what you don't know'. Following the development programme in which the first set of styles and climate data was shared Belron® reran the questionnaire for each executive annually.

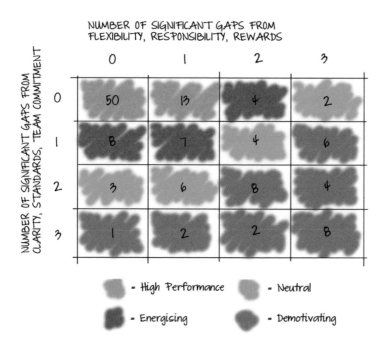

Appendix 3
Belron® is no different from any other organisation

Of executives receiving feedback for the first time, the most popular dominant style in Belron® is democratic (47 per cent of the sample), 37 per cent have the coercive style and 43 per cent the authoritative. Pacesetting is the lowest at 22 per cent. You may recall that a dominant style is one seen by the direct reports as recurring leadership behaviour. This group (those receiving their first set of data) create a range of climates very similar to the Hay Group benchmark data for 2007. Of them, 40 per cent are de-motivating and 43 per cent produce either an energising or high performance climate.

	FIRST SET OF DATA	HAY BENCHMARK
HIGH PERFORMANCE	27%	26%
ENERGISING	16%	18%
NEUTRAL	17%	15%
DEMOTIVATING	40%	41%

Appendix 4
Personal development focusing on leadership styles (behaviour) has a significant impact on the climate created for direct reports

For the executives still employed at December 2009 their latest data shows 50 per cent more are dominant in the authoritative style; the number dominant in the coercive style has fallen by 41 per cent and pacesetting by 28 per cent. The number dominant in the other resonant styles has risen. Goleman, Boyatzis and McKee describe the authoritative, affiliative, democratic and coaching styles as resonant, and coercive and pacesetting styles as dissonant.[3]

There was a dramatic improvement in the climate created. Their latest data showed 70 per cent create either energising or high performance climates compared to 42 per cent in their first set of data and just 14 per cent create a de-motivating climate compared with 41 per cent.

	FIRST SET OF DATA	LAST SET OF DATA
HIGH PERFORMANCE	28%	53%
ENERGISING	14%	17%
NEUTRAL	17%	16%
DEMOTIVATING	41%	14%

Execs in post at end of the research period

Coaching and development work with executives focused on strengthening the resonant styles, in particular authoritative and coaching, and reducing use of the dissonant styles. Whilst it's climate that directly influences results, the focus was on the styles, the behaviours. My experience was that executives want to make development plans around climate dimensions but those making the most progress focus on the root cause, leadership styles.

Appendix 5
Improved self-awareness has made a big contribution to leadership development
Overall, the self-awareness of this group (those still employed at December 2009) improved by 12 per cent. The Hay Group tool compares the leaders' views on what styles they intended to use with the perception of direct reports.

This contrasts with a 3 per cent decline in self-awareness for the group of leavers.

For country general managers self-awareness improved by 19 per cent.

Appendix 9 summarises the extremely poor self-awareness of those leading by solely telling or showing, the dissonant styles.

Appendix 6
As Belron® focuses on leadership, the expectations of the leaders' teams grow
The ideal climate demanded by direct reports has risen by 2.5 per cent when comparing the first and last sets of data for those in post at December 2009.

The challenge for executives was to close a gap that was widening simply because the expectations of leaders were increasing.

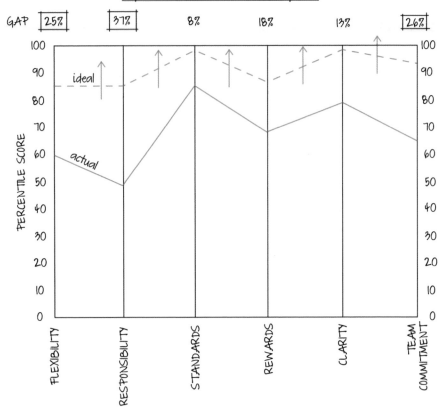

Expectations (Ideal) Have Risen by 2.5%

GAP   [25%]   [37%]   8%   18%   13%   [26%]

Appendix 7
Belron® keeps leaders who create the better climates

For leavers (irrespective of reason), their last set of data showed that 54 per cent created a de-motivating climate, compared with 42 per cent in their first set of data.

	Leavers	Still Employed
High Performance	27%	53%
Energising	14%	17%
Neutral	5%	16%
Demotivating	54%	14%

There is a stark contrast in the climates created by executives still in post compared to those who left.

Appendix 8
The nine members of the senior team (those with the biggest influence on business results) led by example, although as a group their first set of data was no better than the Hay Group benchmark

Looking at just the senior team, the CEO and his direct reports, the latest set of data shows all of them creating energising or high performance climates, compared with 33 per cent in their first set of data. Eight are dominant in the authoritative style. Again, this group's first set of climate data was similar to the Hay Group benchmark of 2007.

Senior Team

	FIRST SET OF DATA	LAST SET OF DATA
HIGH PERFORMANCE	2	5
ENERGISING	1	4
NEUTRAL	2	0
DEMOTIVATING	4	0

It's a similar picture for the general manager population, the number dominant in the resonant styles increasing and declining for the dissonant. There's a big improvement, 19 per cent, in self-awareness of the styles. Also, 68 per cent create an energising or high performance climate compared with 44 per cent in their first set of data.

General Managers

	FIRST SET OF DATA	LAST SET OF DATA
HIGH PERFORMANCE	28%	48%
ENERGISING	16%	20%
NEUTRAL	20%	24%
DEMOTIVATING	36%	8%

Appendix 9

*Those with only pacesetting or coercive styles are effectively blind to both
the styles they are using and their perceived strength in the resonant styles*

I looked at leaders dominant in one style only. For executives having just the
coercive style as the dominant one, none created a high performance climate
and just 5 per cent an energising climate. Self-awareness was extremely poor. A
whopping 98 per cent believed they were less coercive than their direct reports
experienced; the other 2 per cent were accurate in their assessment. And 87 per
cent believed they were more authoritative than their direct reports, as did 89 per
cent for both affiliative and democratic and 80 per cent for coaching.

There's a similar picture for those only dominant in the pacesetting style. Of
those, 90 per cent thought they were less pacesetting, 88 per cent believed they
were more authoritative than their team, 84 per cent more democratic and affiliative
and 80 per cent more coaching than their direct reports perceived.

The 'Tell' and 'Show' Leadership Approach Leaves Leaders Blind to the Impact they have

	LEAD BY TELLING ONLY	LEAD BY SHOWING ONLY
BLIND TO THE STYLE THEY USE	98%	90%
BELIEVE THEY USE RESONANT LEADERSHIP STYLES BUT DO NOT	86%	84%

Appendix 10

*A range of resonant styles is necessary to create the best climate to produce
results; on their own they are not as powerful as the four in combination*

For the group dominant in all the resonant styles (authoritative, affiliative, democratic and coaching) only one created a de-motivating climate, whilst 88 per cent
create energising or high performance climates.

By analysing groups dominant in only one of the resonant styles it's clear
that the combination of all four resonant styles is required to create the best

climate. The following table demonstrates the impact of the four resonant styles in combination compared with the best climate created by just a single resonant style on each of the climate dimensions.

% Execs with No Gap Greater than 20%

	FOUR RESONANT STYLES	STRONGEST SINGLE STYLE
FLEXIBILITY	86%	51%
RESPONSIBILITY	95%	86%
STANDARDS	89%	88%
REWARDS	91%	37%
CLARITY	89%	63%
TEAM COMMITMENT	92%	64%

Being strong in just one aspect of leadership is clearly not enough. In the same way, it's the complete range of winning behaviours that creates the impact on others that drives performance. The matrix (Fig 7.2) in Chapter 7 demonstrates this point.

Appendix 11
Coaching on styles to which leaders are generally blind improves self-awareness (and the climates leaders create)
Self-awareness of those being coached improved by 21 per cent on use of the coercive style (compared with an 8 per cent improvement for executives still employed) and 8 per cent on use of the pacesetting style (compared with a decline in self-awareness of 10 per cent for executives still employed).

Of individuals that moved from creating a de-motivating to a high performance climate, 93 per cent had a coach to support them.

Appendix 12.
The link between climate and results

Hay Group research indicates that climate accounts for as much as much as 30 per cent of the variation in performance. Belron® looked at roles that were common across all the business units and selected a regional manager, someone who is responsible for a number of stores or outlets. The link between climate and performance was clear. Energising and high performance climates were created by the four resonant styles and an absence of the two dissonant. For neutral and de-motivating styles the opposite was true: low use of the resonant styles and high use of the dissonant styles.

A regional manager is four times more likely to deliver above average profit performance if they create a high performance or energising climate.

Of all the things a regional manager could be encouraged to focus on, none was more compelling than developing his own leadership capability. It's a great opportunity to deliver better results.

There's a common measure for the effectiveness of finance directors across the Belron® Group based on timeliness and accuracy of accounts. Again, the recurring theme was that better performers create better climates.

Over a six-year period the climates generated by the finance directors in twenty business units were compared with their effectiveness in the role. Those generating energising or high performance climates had an average rank of 8th, whilst the neutral and de-motivating had an average ranking of 12th (out of 20).

Houldsworth and Machin published further evidence in 'Leadership Team Performance Management: The Case of Belron®', in which improvement in climate is linked to the performance of two business units (countries) and a central function.[4]

Finally the annual composite climate (percentage of executives with a high performance or energising climate) is plotted below against growth in sales and profit. Again the link to performance is clear. It was widely acknowledged in Belron® that leadership was a key component to growing the business profitably. With identical senior roles in so many countries anecdotal evidence was widely available.

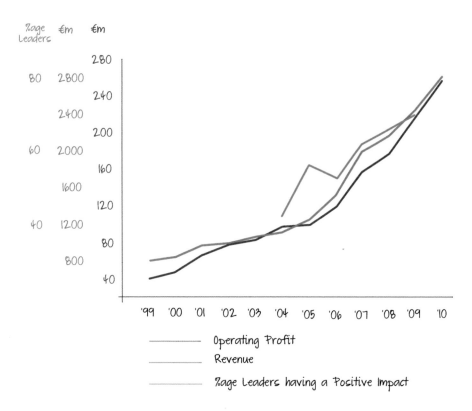

Operating Profit

Revenue

%age Leaders having a Positive Impact

Appendix 13

Climate experienced by direct reports
is not enough to measure leadership capability

Whilst the styles and climate tool had a profound impact on the quality of leadership in Belron®, it is only part of the picture. Firstly, it is a ninety degree tool, in that climate is experienced only by those who are direct reports to the leader. Secondly, it misses elements of emotional intelligence competencies, which is why the Hay Group has other tools to measure those dimensions of leadership. Finally, it provides only a score; it lacks the richness that narrative feedback provides.

By analysing separately three hundred and sixty degree feedback based on a traditional competency framework that incorporated the emotional intelligence dimensions I was able to get the full picture for my research and most importantly the comprehensive examples that bring the winning behaviours to life.

Appendix 14
The Belron® competencies

Belron® has nine competencies and five emotional intelligence (EI) drivers, which are used to differentiate high performing executives. These competencies were applied consistently in recruitment, development and performance measurement throughout the period of research.

SUMMARY OF COMPETENCY DEFINITIONS & EI DRIVERS

Strategic Outlook is the ability to understand the wider vision and strategy (rather than just for a personal area of responsibility) and to translate this understanding into a clear strategic direction. It requires the individual to relate to goals and to see what these require in the local market. Strategic Outlook involves planning for the long term, ensuring that actions are aligned day-to-day with the mission, and knowing how to pace the evolution of a strategy over time.

Commercial Insight means continuously assessing the external environment, analysing the impact of these factors on BELRON® as a whole and their specific impact on the business unit/function and deciding what to do. It is demonstrated by an understanding of the relationship between cost, quality and service delivery and by an effective balancing of all three into practical business plans. Commercial Insight involves analytic and conceptual thinking, and timely action on the basis of incomplete information.

Push for Results is a personal desire and energy to succeed against high standards. It means not just wanting to achieve tough business goals, but also continuously striving for improvement and creating or grasping opportunities to attain excellence. At the highest levels, Push for Results involves taking calculated entrepreneurial risks to make step changes in business performance for BELRON® and being willing to take decisive action now in anticipation of future opportunities or problems.

Innovation means having an open-minded approach to the business and demonstrating a willingness to challenge existing ways of doing things in the interests of better business results. It involves thinking creatively about all areas of the business and having the self-confidence to champion new ideas, even when these may be contentious. Innovation means actively embracing the application of new forms of technology and creating a climate within the business unit that encourages and rewards initiative and value adding activity from all employees.

Customer Focus is the desire to give world class service to customers. It means not only seeing through their eyes and meeting their needs, but also knowing what customers will want before they do. It requires ensuring that the business unit is outwardly focused towards the market and that the energies of all BELRON® employees are harnessed towards delivering 100 per cent customer satisfaction. Customer Focus also means establishing systems to monitor customer satisfaction and brand awareness and ensuring that this information drives developments in the business.

Partnership is the ability to develop and sustain effective long-term coalitions and relationships with key customers, specifiers, suppliers, the media and others who are critical to achieving superior business performance for BELRON®. It involves being able to influence the thinking and actions of others, to operate at many levels within organisations, to understand their concerns and how they make decisions, to spot and develop 'win-win' solutions and to build social and informal relationships and strategies.

Teamworking is the desire to work cooperatively with others across the business. It means being genuinely interested in the success of the whole enterprise, not just one's own area of responsibility. It calls for behaviour that challenges others in a constructive way, and for creating horizontal channels of communication. Teamworking also means proactively sharing insights and knowledge across the wider team in order that others may learn from experiences and mistakes.

Leading Others is the ability to articulate and communicate the BELRON®/business unit vision and to inspire and motivate others in achieving that vision. It involves the capacity to win emotional commitment to the company, colleagues and work. It reflects a drive to provide clarity of direction, set high standards for performance and model the behaviour associated with commitment and success. Leading Others implies empowering others to act and holding them accountable for outcomes. It also includes an ability to energise a team to commit to stretching goals in line with the business strategy.

Developing Talent is a genuine intent to support the learning and development of others, with attention to how their talents can best be utilised to meet the needs of BELRON® and to further their personal career success. It involves creating an environment that encourages and rewards investment in people at all levels, but also refusing poor performance. Additionally, Developing Talent requires focusing on and committing energy and time to growing oneself.

Self Awareness is the ability to recognise one's emotions and their effects. It is the ability to effectively read how we react to cues in the environment and be aware of how one's emotions affect performance.

Self-Assessment is being aware of one's strengths and limitations. It is based on the desire to receive feedback and new perspectives about oneself and to be motivated by continuous learning and self-development. It implies having the ability to target areas for change.

Self-Confidence is a belief in one's own capability to accomplish a task and select an effective approach to a task or problem. This includes confidence in one's ability as expressed in increasingly challenging circumstances and confidence in one's decisions or opinions.

Managing Own Emotions is the ability to keep one's impulsive feelings and emotions under control and restrain negative actions when provoked, when faced with opposition or hostility from others, or when working under pressure. It also includes the ability to maintain stamina under continuing stress.

Empathy is having the ability to understand other people. It is the ability to accurately hear and understand the unspoken or partly expressed thoughts, feelings, and concerns of others. It implies taking an active interest in other people's concerns. It measures increasing complexity and depth of understanding of others and may include cross-cultural sensitivity.

The enthusiasm shown by executives for elements of the styles and climate tool provided by Hay Group – in particular the fact that a dimension of leadership can be measured – was one of the reasons that prompted us to re-look at the performance review tool in 2006.

There were concerns that climate, because it is the perspective of only direct reports, was not providing the complete picture. Whilst not commonplace, there were examples of executives who created an outstanding climate but their boss was occasionally getting a different message from feedback in the three hundred and sixty degree performance review. In other words, the boss themselves, peers and other groups (other than the executive's own team) sometimes had a different perspective.

There's more to leadership than just managing your direct reports. It also involves influencing positively upwards, across and sometimes beyond the organisation.

As a consequence the performance review process was refreshed to include

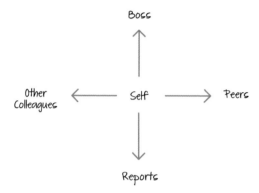

an assessment of strength demonstrated against the competencies and EI drivers across the various dimensions of leadership, including a self-assessment. A level of 85 per cent was set to describe 'world class' in a competency. Belron® retained a request for narrative feedback that provides richness beyond just a rating. The quality of feedback steadily improved over time.

What was clear from the Hay Group leadership styles data was, firstly, that self-awareness of behaviour is an issue and, secondly, that it's key to improvement. There were significant differences between the leaders' view on the style they were using and the perspective of those on the receiving end. Self-awareness is, however, just one of many emotional intelligence competencies. The table below shows how these are comprehensively covered in the Belron® performance review.

As a consequence, and fortunately from my point of view, the performance review covers emotional intelligence competencies as well as traditional leadership competencies. I had details of both the rating and, most importantly, narrative feedback on all elements. It gave me the complete picture and from all perspectives.

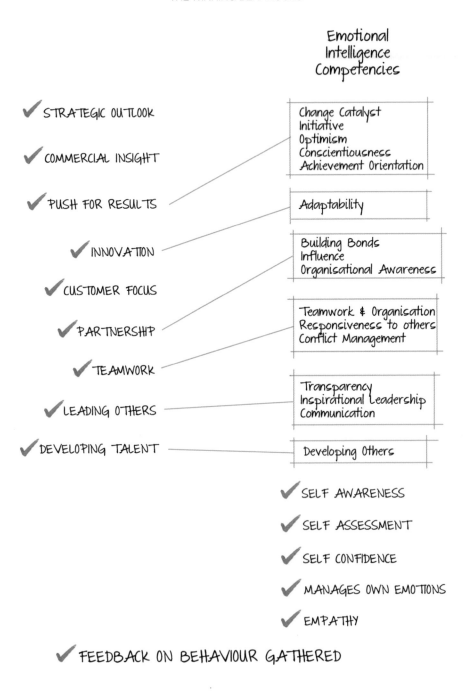

Emotional
Intelligence
Competencies

✓ STRATEGIC OUTLOOK

✓ COMMERCIAL INSIGHT

✓ PUSH FOR RESULTS

✓ INNOVATION

✓ CUSTOMER FOCUS

✓ PARTNERSHIP

✓ TEAMWORK

✓ LEADING OTHERS

✓ DEVELOPING TALENT

Change Catalyst
Initiative
Optimism
Conscientiousness
Achievement Orientation

Adaptability

Building Bonds
Influence
Organisational Awareness

Teamwork & Organisation
Responsiveness to others
Conflict Management

Transparency
Inspirational Leadership
Communication

Developing Others

✓ SELF AWARENESS

✓ SELF ASSESSMENT

✓ SELF CONFIDENCE

✓ MANAGES OWN EMOTIONS

✓ EMPATHY

✓ FEEDBACK ON BEHAVIOUR GATHERED

Appendix 15
Measuring leadership capability
Belron® assessed leadership quality by the number of competencies an executive was rated 'world class' in by all giving feedback (except themselves).
Similar to the climate matrix, this demonstrates the stretch in the measure.

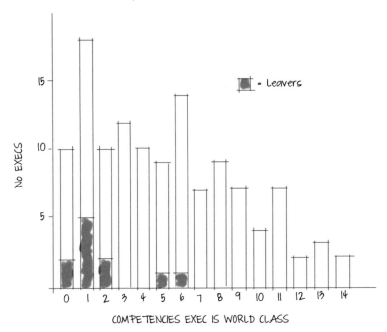

COMPETENCIES EXEC IS WORLD CLASS

Appendix 16
The positive behaviours associated with resonant styles overlap with the behaviours demonstrated by world class leaders in the broader range of leadership and emotional intelligence competencies
There is a correlation between executives who are in the upper quartile for their three hundred and sixty degree performance review and the quality of the climate they created. Of those in the upper quartile, only two have not gathered styles and climate feedback (because they do not have direct reports), 74 per cent create high performance climates, and none a de-motivating climate. That's not really surprising as half the feedback was from direct reports in the performance review and the resonant styles that create good climate are likely to be viewed positively by others as well.

Appendix 17

There's more to winning behaviours than just Hay Group's leadership styles, although they do play a large part

I focused on executives who were rated 90 per cent or over (beyond the Belron® world class definition of 85 per cent) on any particular competency and recorded verbatim comments on both the behaviour and impact on others.

Executives rated this highly provided a sample of feedback from 1400 individuals around the leader.

I compared feedback on behaviours from the performance review that are directly attributable to one of Hay Group's definitions of leadership styles.

The Links between Winning Behaviours and Hay Group Styles

	%
COERCIVE	0.3
AUTHORITATIVE	19.7
AFFILIATIVE	10.7
DEMOCRATIC	9.1
PACESETTING	5.2
COACHING	13.7
	58.7

Of the winning behaviours, 59 per cent could be directly attributable to the Hay Group definition of styles, with authoritative the most prevalent at 19.7 per cent and the dissonant styles of pacesetting, 5.2 per cent, and coercive, 0.3 per cent, being the least frequently seen.

What's missing?

There was a range of behaviours that described how an executive used or managed their emotions positively through a thorough knowledge of them. Leaders' relative intelligence and ability to think analytically clearly plays a part. The remaining feedback can best be described as generic leadership behaviour, but behaviour that is appreciated and seen widely. Openness, listening, networking and being supportive were the most common.

I analysed all the feedback comments into thirty-four recurring themes and

The Winning Behaviours

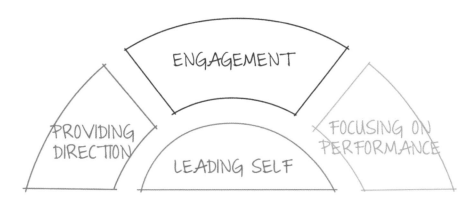

those in turn into the four clusters of winning behaviours: providing direction, engagement, focus on performance and leading self.

Additionally I researched the losing behaviours associated with executives who left for performance reasons.

Of the feedback comments, 49 per cent could be directly attributed to the Hay leadership styles, lower than the winning behaviour percentage. The mix was very different.

The impact is as much from what people perceive is missing.

The Links between Losing Behaviours and Hay Group Styles

	Presence (%)	Absence (%)
COERCIVE	13.4	–
AUTHORITATIVE	–	7.8
AFFILIATIVE	2.2	4.8
DEMOCRATIC	0.4	4.8
PACESETTING	12.6	1.5
COACHING	–	2.2
	28.6	21.1

Hence my conclusion:

Winning behaviours and the avoidance of losing behaviours represent a synthesis of the Hay Group resonant and dissonant styles, emotional intelligence competencies and the leadership associated with traditional competency frameworks. Winning behaviours are based on the perception of everyone around the leader; the research is three hundred and sixty degrees. In that sense it is comprehensive.

Appendix 18

World class customer focus amongst executives is perceived as leaders who can put customer service in the context of corporate vision rather than someone who can step into the customers' shoes

There's a strong correlation between some of the original nine leadership competencies and specific Hay Group leadership styles.

From the definitions two are clearly linked: strategic outlook to the authoritative style and developing talent to the coaching style. The third is more interesting, though. Ratings on the Belron® leadership competency customer focus correlate strongly with the authoritative style. An analysis of feedback on executives who rated over 90 per cent on this competency reveals that 5 per cent gave examples of executives who put themselves in their customers' shoes or who engaged personally with customers. The vast majority of comments put customer service for others into a strategic perspective, demonstrating enthusiasm for all aspects of service or seeking a thorough analysis of customer needs. That's what we've described as providing direction in Chapter 2.

I conclude from this that if customer service is important in your organisation it's either an output like profit or cash flow or, for executives, an integral part of explaining how it fits into the organisation's vision.

For customer facing roles I'm sure that being empathetic and putting yourself in the customer's shoes are key behaviours, but that's clearly not the case for executives. Their role and behaviour should be very different.

Appendix 19

The link between leadership and results

Throughout the period 2000 to 2010 Belron® gathered qualitative feedback against leadership competencies for all its executives worldwide. In 2007 the performance review tool was refreshed to include scores as well as narrative feedback. From 2002 Belron® gathered styles and climate data for all its executives. Lots of organisations gather feedback on emotional intelligence, on competencies, and some also use the Hay Group tool of styles and climate. What differentiates Belron® is the genuine belief that leadership really makes a difference and the relentless quest for individual improvement; it actively encourages leaders to develop because Belron® believes that leadership provides a competitive edge. There is an output to leadership. Both Houldsworth and Jirasinghe[5] and Gobillot[6] recognise the link from leadership to results at Belron®.

Throughout the period of the research Belron® focused on a number of priorities: the sharing of best practice and managing change, particularly when integrating acquisitions. Its vision of profitable growth through being the natural choice for customers remained unchanged. Leadership was always a Belron® priority. Without it the business results would not have been so remarkable.

From 1999, the year the competency framework was launched, to 2010 Belron® consistently grew profit at a greater rate than sales: profitable growth. It recorded compound sales growth of 12 per cent and profit of 18 per cent.

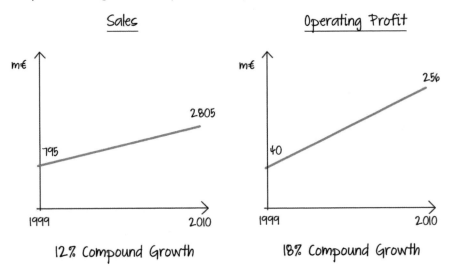

Appendix 20
Creating a winning behaviours diagnostic
The summary of questions at the end of Chapters 2 through to 7 can be used as a template to create a leadership diagnostic.

I recommend seven sections to the diagnostic. The number of questions in each is in brackets.

Impact on Performance (1)
Providing Direction (6)

Engagement (8)

Focus on Performance (14)

Leading Self (6)

Losing Behaviours (6)

Impact on Others (9)

That's fifty questions in total. The performance question is important because there is a purpose, an output to leadership. Over time, as you gather more data, the links we have explored in this book from behaviours to the impact on others and finally performance will become clear.

At the end of each section there should be the opportunity for some narrative feedback. A question prompts people to think why they see some aspects of leadership as being stronger than others.

The questionnaire would look something like this:

WINNING BEHAVIOURS QUESTIONNAIRE

The quality of the feedback gathered plays a significant part in improving our understanding of both what we do and where we can improve. The best examples of feedback state what you see or hear followed by the impact that has either on yourself or others. For example: "One of my team was thrilled to get a call to congratulate him, it was very motivational"; "He can be too verbose and the key messages get lost as people switch off".

<u>How Characteristic are the Following for the Leader being Evauated?</u>

IMPACT ON PERFORMANCE

	VERY NEGATIVE		NEUTRAL		VERY POSITIVE	DON'T KNOW
THINKING ABOUT THE INDIVIDUAL'S OVERALL PERFORMANCE AND IMPACT ON KEY PERFORMANCE INDICATORS HOW DO YOU RANK THEIR PERFORMANCE	☐	☐	☐	☐	☐	☐

When you answered the above question what examples were you thinking about when you responded as you did?

How Characteristic are the Following for the Leader being Evaluated?

PROVIDING DIRECTION

	NOT AT ALL		SOMEWHAT		VERY	DON'T KNOW
COMMUNICATES FREQUENTLY AND CONSISTENTLY A CLEAR SENSE OF DIRECTION	☐	☐	☐	☐	☐	☐
FOCUSES ON PRIORITIES	☐	☐	☐	☐	☐	☐
BUILDS COMMITMENT AND ENCOURAGES ACTION TOWARDS A VISION OR STRATEGY	☐	☐	☐	☐	☐	☐
ENSURES ALIGNMENT BOTH WITH OTHERS AND ORGANISATIONAL STRATEGY	☐	☐	☐	☐	☐	☐
DEMONSTRATES COMMERCIAL INSIGHT THINKS QUICKLY AND ANALYTICALLY	☐	☐	☐	☐	☐	☐
SHOWS A THIRST FOR KNOWLEDGE AND INSIGHTS	☐	☐	☐	☐	☐	☐

When you answered the above question what examples were you thinking about when you responded as you did?

How Characteristic are the Following
for the Leader being Evaluated?

ENGAGEMENT

	NOT AT ALL		SOMEWHAT		VERY	DON'T KNOW
LISTENS ATTENTIVELY	☐	☐	☐	☐	☐	☐
SHOWS CONSIDERATION FOR THE FEELINGS AND NEEDS OF OTHERS	☐	☐	☐	☐	☐	☐
SEEKS AND CONSIDERS THE VIEWS AND OPINIONS OF OTHERS	☐	☐	☐	☐	☐	☐
INVESTS TIME TO CREATE AND MAINTAIN NETWORKS	☐	☐	☐	☐	☐	☐
SHARES RELEVANT INFORMATION, KEEPS PEOPLE UPDATED	☐	☐	☐	☐	☐	☐
WORKS COLLABORATIVELY WITH OTHERS, A TEAM WORKER	☐	☐	☐	☐	☐	☐
BUILDS RAPPORT AND EMOTIONAL COMMITMENT	☐	☐	☐	☐	☐	☐
IS TRANSPARENT, OPEN, TRUSTWORTHY	☐	☐	☐	☐	☐	☐

When you answered the above question what examples were you thinking about when you responded as you did?

Appendices

<u>How Characteristic are the Following
for the Leader being Evaluated?</u>

FOCUS ON PERFORMANCE

	NOT AT ALL		SOMEWHAT		VERY	DON'T KNOW
ENCOURAGES OTHERS TO ACT AND TAKE RESPONSIBILITY	☐	☐	☐	☐	☐	☐
ENCOURAGES NEW IDEAS AND WAYS OF LOOKING AT THINGS	☐	☐	☐	☐	☐	☐
PUTS ENERGY, TIME AND FOCUS INTO PERSONAL COACHING	☐	☐	☐	☐	☐	☐
REMOVES BARRIERS, CREATES SPACE AND OPPORTUNITY TO DEVELOP	☐	☐	☐	☐	☐	☐
ACCURATELY ASSESSES STRENGTHS AND WEAKNESSES OF OTHERS	☐	☐	☐	☐	☐	☐
PROVIDES CONSTRUCTIVE IMPACTFUL FEEDBACK	☐	☐	☐	☐	☐	☐
FOCUSED ON DELIVERY AND THE RELENTLESS PURSUIT OF GOALS	☐	☐	☐	☐	☐	☐
MAKES APPROPRIATE RECOMMENDATIONS	☐	☐	☐	☐	☐	☐
SETS CLEAR STANDARDS AND HIGH EXPECTATIONS	☐	☐	☐	☐	☐	☐
REWARDS PERFORMANCE	☐	☐	☐	☐	☐	☐
ADVOCATES THE SHARING OF BEST PRACTICE	☐	☐	☐	☐	☐	☐
TACKLES POOR PERFORMANCE	☐	☐	☐	☐	☐	☐
PROVIDES TIMELY AND CONSTRUCTIVE CHALLENGE	☐	☐	☐	☐	☐	☐
SEES THE VALUE OF PERSONAL DEVELOPMENT	☐	☐	☐	☐	☐	☐

When you answered the above question what examples were you thinking about when you responded as you did?

Appendices

How Characteristic are the Following for the Leader being Evaluated?

LEADING SELF

	NOT AT ALL		SOMEWHAT		VERY	DON'T KNOW
ACTIVELY SEEKS AND IS RECEPTIVE TO FEEDBACK	☐	☐	☐	☐	☐	☐
ACCURATELY ASSESSES THEIR OWN STRENGTHS AND WEAKNESSES	☐	☐	☐	☐	☐	☐
AWARE OF THEIR PERSONAL TRIGGERS	☐	☐	☐	☐	☐	☐
CHANNELS THEIR EMOTIONS TO HAVE A POSITIVE IMPACT	☐	☐	☐	☐	☐	☐
DEMONSTRATES CONFIDENCE IN THEMSELVES TO PERFORM	☐	☐	☐	☐	☐	☐
HAS A POSITIVE OUTLOOK, ENTHUSIASTIC, ENERGETIC AND SHOWS AMBITION	☐	☐	☐	☐	☐	☐

When you answered the above question what examples were you thinking about when you responded as you did?

How Characteristic are the Following
for the Leader being Evaluated?

LOSING BEHAVIOURS

	NOT AT ALL		SOMEWHAT		VERY	DON'T KNOW
TELLS OR SHOWS OTHERS WHAT TO DO	☐	☐	☐	☐	☐	☐
AVOIDS CONTACT WITH OTHERS AND OPERATES IN A SILO	☐	☐	☐	☐	☐	☐
APPEARS INFLEXIBLE, DEFENSIVE AND RISK AVERSE	☐	☐	☐	☐	☐	☐
FOCUSES ONLY ON THEIR OWN AGENDA	☐	☐	☐	☐	☐	☐
GETS IMMERSED IN DETAIL	☐	☐	☐	☐	☐	☐
EXPRESSES FRUSTRATION WITH OTHERS AND EVENTS	☐	☐	☐	☐	☐	☐

When you answered the above question what examples were you thinking about when you responded as you did?

How do you Rate this Individual's Impact
on you and others?

	DISAGREE STRONGLY		SOMEWHAT AGREE		AGREE STRONGLY	DON'T KNOW
PROVIDES THE CLARITY REQUIRED FOR PEOPLE TO DO THEIR BEST	☐	☐	☐	☐	☐	☐
CARES ABOUT PEOPLE AND CREATES OPEN AND TRUSTING RELATIONSHIPS	☐	☐	☐	☐	☐	☐
CREATES A SENSE OF TEAM SPIRIT	☐	☐	☐	☐	☐	☐
MOTIVATES AND INSPIRES OTHERS TO DO THEIR BEST WORK	☐	☐	☐	☐	☐	☐
EMPOWERS OTHERS AND MAKES THEM ACCOUNTABLE	☐	☐	☐	☐	☐	☐
CONTRIBUTES TO THE PERSONAL DEVELOPMENT OF OTHERS	☐	☐	☐	☐	☐	☐
PROVIDES CONFIDENCE TO OTHERS THROUGH WORKING WITH HIM/HER	☐	☐	☐	☐	☐	☐
CREATES APPROPRIATE CALMNESS IN POTENTIALLY STRESSFUL SITUATIONS	☐	☐	☐	☐	☐	☐
DOES NOT CREATE UNNECESSARY PRESSURE TO PERFORM	☐	☐	☐	☐	☐	☐

When you answered the above question what examples were you thinking about when you responded as you did?

As discussed in Chapter 8 we would want to get feedback from everyone around the leader, including a self-review. Consequently the line manager would complete the questionnaire himself and request input from the person being reviewed as well as direct reports and colleagues or peers of the person being reviewed. Including three or more people in each of the last two groups will ensure anonymity.

If you are gathering feedback directly, rather than through your line manager, the challenge for you is to overcome the barriers to others being open and honest with their comments and assessment. The request for feedback needs to make clear your genuine desire to hear both what you are doing right and what you could do better. Think about the Johari window – which approach is going to encourage comments about your blind spots in the behaviours you use?

When everyone has responded you will have a comprehensive set of feedback to create a report. Simply cut and paste the narrative feedback into the appropriate category. To create a percentage I simply score 0 for don't know, minus 1 for not at all characteristic, followed by 1, 2 (somewhat characteristic), 3 and 4 (very characteristic).

The important things are to commit to a rerun in a year's time and to be consistent in the way you aggregate scores to produce a rating. You will now have the scores to produce a summary.

I've reproduced below Fig 8.2 (an example of an overall summary) and Fig 8.3 (Providing Direction) as an example of a section in the questionnaire.

I encourage you to use the diagnostic to help understand an individual's leadership strengths and areas for potential improvement. You may recall that a score produces a real incentive to change for some leaders. It also provides a reliable way to track progress. For others, it's the words that prompt a reaction. The winning behaviours diagnostic will provide you with both.

I produced the diagnostic initially to design a framework for writing the book. I have since used it in recruitment, when observing candidates, and as a performance management tool. The main attributes are that it is a three hundred and sixty degree tool, it gathers qualitative as well as quantitative data and, critically, it links behaviour through impact on others to an organisational outcome, performance. It takes only an hour to complete.

WINNING BEHAVIOURS SUMMARY

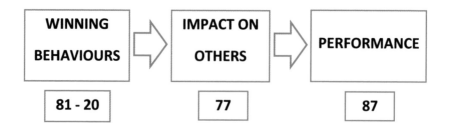

WINNING BEHAVIOURS	IMPACT ON OTHERS	PERFORMANCE
81 - 20	77	87

BEHAVIOURS

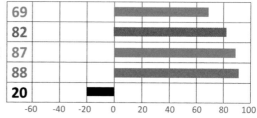

PROVIDING DIRECTION	69
ENGAGEMENT	82
FOCUS ON PERFORMANCE	87
LEADING SELF	88
LOSING	20

IMPACT ON OTHERS

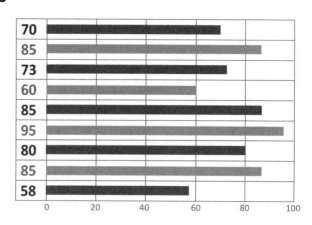

CLARITY	70
THERE FOR ME	85
TEAM SPIRIT	73
MOTIVATED	60
EMPOWERED	85
DEVELOPING ME	95
CONFIDENT	80
CALM	85
STRESS FREE	58

PROVIDING DIRECTION

Self
I rally the team around specific challenges
I can stand back and help people who are bogged down in detail
I constantly remind my team why customer retention is so important

Line Manager
He gains insights from many sources and shares to improve overall understanding
Regularly shares the company vision
His plans are always linked to company strategy

Direct Reports
Through constant reinforcement we are clear what we are doing and why
Short term actions are always linked to longer term goals
Comprehensive analysis keeps us ahead of our competitors

Peers
Sometimes comes across as wanting to demonstrate superior intellect
Could be more demonstrable about the things that matter
Spends too much time worrying about consumer expectations rather than doing something

Others
Seemingly endless curiosity, seeks insights from every part of the business
He has the whole team tuned into our philosophy on quality
He tends to keep the discussion focused on priorities rather than letting it drift.

REFERENCES

Introduction

1. Daniel Goleman, 'Leadership That Gets Results', Harvard Business Review, March–April, 2000. Describes leadership styles and how they link with the dimensions of climate, which, in turn, drive performance.

Chapter 1. Leadership Is Not Part Of Your Job – It *Is* Your Job

1. Elizabeth Houldsworth and Simon Machin, 'Leadership Team Performance: The Case of Belron®', Team Performance Management, Vol. 14, No. 3/4, 2008. Explains the impact climate has on performance and summarises the relevant research.

2. Daniel Goleman, Working with Emotional Intelligence. Page 19 describes the limits of IQ.

3. David C McClelland, 'Testing for competence rather than intelligence', American Psychologist, 1973. Identifies the importance of being able to read emotional messages in people to succeed.

4. Marcus Buckingham and Curt Coffman, First Break All The Rules. Page 67 defines talent, stressing the importance of the word 'recurring' and the key to performance being matching talents to the role.

5. Buckingham and Coffman, as above, note 4. Pages 69–76 describe how talent rather than the conventional wisdom of experience, brainpower or willpower is the critical factor to success.

6. Daniel Goleman, 'What Makes a Leader?' Harvard Business Review, January, 2004 (originally published 1998). Indicates that emotional intelligence is twice as important as intellect or cognitive skills (such as big picture thinking) as a driver of outstanding performance; and positions IQ and technical skills as being insufficient for success.

Chapter 2. A Guiding Star (Providing Direction)

1. Kouzes and Posner, The Leadership Challenge, 4th Edition. Page 30 discusses how what people look for in a leader has been constant over time; and page 103 describes five practices for a good leader, one of which is to inspire a shared vision.

2. Jim Collins, Good to Great. Page 90 describes the hedgehog concept, a thorough understanding of three things, what you're deeply passionate about, what you can be best in the world at and what drives your economic engine.

3. John P Kotter and Dan S Cohen, The Heart of Change. Pages 3–6 summarise the eight stages of successful large-scale change.

4. Frank LaFasto and Carl Larson, When Teams Work Best. Page 107 explains the pitfalls of a leader leaving his team behind.

5. Marcus Buckingham, The One Thing You Need To Know. Page 71 describes the differences between great leaders and managers.

6. Buckingham, as above, note 5. Page 145 describes great leaders as alchemists 'speeding up the reactions between the individuals' talents and the company's goals'.

7. Patrick Lencioni, The Three Signs of a Miserable Job. Pages 231–5 describe irrelevance.

8. Goleman, as Introduction, note 1.

9. Kouzes and Posner, as above, note 1. Page 151 describes how it's difficult to enlist others if you have trouble seeing yourself living the future vision.

10. Stephen Denning, 'Telling Tales', Harvard Business Review, May, 2004. Describes the narrative patterns associated with 'sparking action' and 'leading people into the future'.

11. Stephen R Covey, The Seven Habits of Highly Effective People, 15th anniversary edition. Page 145 describes 'Put[ting] First Things First' as the third principle of personal management.

12. Covey, as above, note 11. Page 161 describes how to manage our lives more effectively.

13. Robert S Kaplan, 'What to Ask the Person in the Mirror', Harvard Business Review, January, 2007. Part of a self-test around visions, priorities and managing time.

14. Emmanuel Gobillot, Hay Group, from facilitation notes produced for a development programme delivered by Belron®.

15. Jacques Horovitz with Anne-Valérie Ohlsson-Corboz, A Dream with a Deadline. Page 149 describes discipline as one of the four cornerstones of continuous execution (trust, support and stretch are the others).

16. Patrick Lencioni, The Five Dysfunctions of a Team. Page 207 describes lack of commitment as one of the dysfunctions.

17. Buckingham, as above, note 5. Page 181 describes the systematic and symbolic actions leaders take.

18. Stephen Denning, The Secret Language of Leadership. Page 27 describes the hidden pattern to the way successful leaders communicate.

19. Dorothy Leonard and Walter Swap, 'Deep Smarts', Harvard Business Review, September, 2004. Describes 'the stuff that produces that mysterious quality, good judgement'.
20. R Meredith Belbin, Management Teams – Why They Succeed or Fail. Pages 54–6 describe in detail.
21. Dale Carnegie, How to Win Friends and Influence People. Page 128 describes how to avoid making enemies.
22. Patrick Lencioni, The Five Temptations of a CEO. Pages 127–8 describe in detail.
23. Daniel Goleman, Richard Boyatzis and Annie McKee, Primal Leadership. Page 27 describes how the neural systems in the brain responsible for intellect and emotions are separate.
24. Jeffrey A Sonnenfeld, 'What Makes Great Boards', Great Harvard Business Review, September, 2002. Indicates that 25 per cent of CEOs claim their board members don't appreciate the complexity of the business they oversee.
25. Buckingham, as above, note 5. Page 69 discusses how to develop a budding leader.
26. Ram Charan, Know-How. Page 55 describes how leaders 'connect the dots' to pinpoint external change.
27. Jim Collins, How the Mighty Fall. Page 43 describes decline in learning orientation as an indicator of the first stage in decline.
28. Lynn R Offermann, 'When Followers Become Toxic', Harvard Business Review, January, 2004. Describes one of six ways to counter wayward influences from followers.
29. LaFasto and Larson, as above, note 4. Page 124 describes a dimension of team leadership, making team members smart about key issues and facts.
30. Lencioni, as above, note 7. Pages 221–3 describe the three elements contributing to a miserable job: irrelevance, anonymity and immeasurement.

Chapter 3. Where I Belong (Engagement)

1. Lynda Gratton and Tamara J Erickson, 'Eight Ways to Build Collaborative Teams', Harvard Business Review, November, 2007. Describes the balance between relationship and task when seeking the 'right' team leader.
2. Lencioni, as Chapter 2, note 7. Page 221 describes one of the three elements contributing to a miserable job.
3. Carnegie, as Chapter 2, note 21. Page 97 describes how to be a good listener and encourage others to talk about themselves.

4. Covey, as Chapter 2, note 11. Pages 239–41 describe empathic listening.
5. Carnegie, as Chapter 2, note 21. Chapter 1 describes the principle 'Don't criticise, condemn or complain' and Chapter 3 the principle 'Arouse an eager want'.
6. Joseph Luft and Harry Ingham, The Johari Window: A Graphic Model of Inter-personal Awareness, 1955. Describes the impact of what's known and not known by both self and others.
7. James O'Toole and Warren Bennis, 'What's Needed Next – A Culture of Candour', Harvard Business Review, June, 2009. Describes how to create transparency by encouraging people to speak truth to power.
8. Robert B Cialdini, 'Harnessing the Power of Persuasion', Harvard Business Review, October, 2001. Describes how expertise, actual or perceived, is a means of persuasion.
9. James K Sebenius, 'Six Habits of Merely Effective Negotiators', Harvard Business Review, April, 2001. Describes neglecting the other side's problem as one of six common mistakes that prevent successful resolution.
10. Carnegie, as Chapter 2, note 21. Page 37 is attributed to Henry Ford.
11. Sebenius, as above, note 9. Describes failing to correct for skewed vision.
12. Nancy Kline, Time to Think. Page 43 describes how the quality of your attention determines the quality of other people's thinking.
13. Kline, as above, note 12. Page 102 describes how to chair brilliant meetings.
14. Gratton and Erickson, as above, note 1. Describing the creation of a gift culture.
15. Malcolm Gladwell, The Tipping Point. Pages 30–34 describe the 'Law of the Few'.
16. Offermann, as Chapter 2, note 28. Explains why majority rules – that is, the pressure to conform rises with the degree of agreement among those around you.
17. Lencioni, as Chapter 2, note 22. Page 117 advises CEOs to overcome the temptation to choose harmony over productive conflict.
18. Collins, as Chapter 2, note 2. Pages 73–80 describe how to create a climate where the truth is heard.
19. LaFasto and Larson, as Chapter 2, note 4. Pages 108–10 describe how to ensure a collaborative climate.
20. LaFasto and Larson, as Chapter 2, note 4. Page 118 describes how to share the process of controlling what issues get discussed, how solutions are formed and how implementation occurs.
21. Gobillot, as Chapter 2, note 14. Describes the story of the ice cream cone,

which Ernest Hamwi invented as his zalabias (round Persian waffles) were sitting on his stall at the St Louis World Fair unsold as the weather was so hot. Seeing Arnold Fornachou, the ice cream man, run out of tubs to put the ice cream in, Ernest rolled up his round hardening waffles into the shape of a cone and sold them to Arnold. Idea generation-Creation-Execution.

22. Robert Goffee and Gareth Jones, 'Why Should Anyone Be Led by You?' Harvard Business Review, September–October, 2000. Describes the importance of being a 'sensor'.

23. Goffee and Jones, as above, note 22. Describes how leaders give people what they need rather than what they want.

24. Kouzes and Posner, as Chapter 2, note 1. Page 30 describes honesty as the most common characteristic of leaders in surveys from 1987 to 2007.

25. O'Toole and Bennis, as above, note 7. Describes the importance of trustworthiness.

26. Covey, as Chapter 2, note 11. Pages 188–90 describe six ways to make a deposit in an 'emotional bank account'.

27. Collins, as Chapter 2, note 2. Page 78 describes one of four elements in creating a climate where the truth is heard.

28. Lencioni, as Chapter 2, note 16. Page 197 summarises the importance of trust in teams.

29. Covey, as Chapter 2, note 11. Page 270 illustrates how closely trust is related to different levels of communication.

30. Goleman, as Introduction, note 1

31. Carnegie, as Chapter 2, note 21. Page 96 describes how to be a good listener and encourage others to talk about themselves.

32. Kline, as above, note 12. Page 134 describes how today's leader must prize the minds of people above all else.

Chapter 4. In The Zone (Focus on Performance)

1. John Whitmore, Coaching for Performance, 3rd edition. Page 54 describes the sequence in which to ask questions when coaching. Also Max Landsberg, The Tao of Coaching. Page 31 discusses how to structure a coaching session.

2. Daniel H Pink, Drive. Pages 85–108 explore the essential elements of autonomy (task, time, technique and team) and evidence that companies offering autonomy outperform.

3. Paul Strebel, New Compacts for Change. Strebel's model has two axes showing the potential impact of change (vertical, positive and negative) and the energy

(horizontal, passive and active). From this he plots four types of people: change agents, bystanders, traditionalists and resistors.

4. Scott W Spreier, Mary H Fontaine and Ruth L Malloy, 'Leadership Run Amok', Harvard Business Review, June. 2006. Describes three motives and summarises how each impacts a leader's behaviour.
5. Buckingham and Coffman, as Chapter 1, note 4. Page 54 describes the speeding up of a reaction between two substances (an individual's talent and the company goal) to achieve a desired outcome (performance).
6. Buckingham and Coffman, as Chapter 1, note 4. Page 51 summarises the one insight echoed by tens of thousands of great managers.
7. Laura Morgan Roberts, Gretchen Spreitzer, Jane Dutton, Robert Quinn, Emily Heaphy and Brianna Barker, 'How to Play to Your Strengths', Harvard Business Review, January, 2005. Research shows people pay keen attention to negative information, hence the lack of enthusiasm for performance reviews.
8. Carnegie, as Chapter 2, note 21. Page 31 summarises the impact of honest and sincere appreciation.
9. LaFasto and Larson, as Chapter 2, note 4. Page 32 presents evidence to indicate that giving and receiving feedback is critical to building productive team relationships.
10. Luft and Ingham, as Chapter 3, note 6.
11. Jess Lair, I Ain't Much Baby – But I'm All I Got. Page 248.
12. Carnegie, as Chapter 2, note 21. Page 233 describes how leaders spur people on to success.
13. Collins, as Chapter 2, note 2. Page 127 describes how people in good-to-great companies become somewhat extreme in the fulfilment of their responsibilities.
14. Pink, as above, note 2. Page 207; page 120 explains that flow doesn't guarantee mastery.
15. Helen Murlis and Peggy Schubert, Hay Insight, Engage Employees and Boost Performance, 2002. Explains what engagement looks like. References Mihalyi Csikzentmihalyi, Flow: The Psychology of Optimal Experience.
16. Pink, as above, note 2. Pages 120–23 describe the mindset. Page 126 demonstrates that mastery is an asymptote, something you can aim for and get very close to without actually getting there.
17. Buckingham, as Chapter 2, note 5. Page 76 describes one of the four skills managers must use to avoid failure.
18. Gobillot as Chapter 2, note 14.
19. Lencioni, as Chapter 2, note 16. Pages 212–13 describe the willingness of team

members to call their peers on performance or behaviours.

20. Kouzes and Posner, Encouraging the Heart. Page 18 summarises; pages 36–7 provide an encouragement index to assess relative strength.
21. Lencioni, as Chapter 2, note 22. Pages 126–7 summarise.
22. David Cottrell and Mark Layton, The Manager's Coaching Handbook. Page 20 has a checklist.
23. Goleman, Boyatzis and McKee, as Chapter 2, note 23. Pages 59–63 explain the one-to-one coaching style; pages 72–5 describe the pacesetting style.

Chapter 5. Inner Strength (Leading Self)

1. Covey, as Chapter 2, note 11. Page 96 has a quote attributed to Oliver Wendell Holmes; page 53 introduces the seven habits paradigm.
2. Michelle Burckle, Hay Group, research on emotional competency data in 1999.
3. Arbinger Institute, Leadership and Self-Deception. Pages 64–80 describe self-betrayal; pages 81–90 describe life 'in the box'.
4. Luft and Ingham, as Chapter 3, note 6.
5. Jay M. Jackman and Myra H. Strober, 'Fear of Feedback', Harvard Business Review, April, 2003. Describes how to recognise and counter fear of feedback.
6. Goleman, Boyatzis and McKee, as Chapter 2, note 23. Pages 92–6 explain CEO disease.
7. Luft and Ingham, as Chapter 3, note 6.
8. Richard Boyatzis, Annie McKee and Daniel Goleman, 'Reawakening Your Passion for Work', Harvard Business Review, April, 2002. Describes leaders 'taking stock'.
9. Covey, as Chapter 2, note 11. Page 287 introduces balanced self-renewal.
10. Lencioni, as Chapter 2, note 22. Page 118 offers advice for CEOs to trust others with their reputation and ego.
11. Buckingham, as Chapter 2, note 5. Page 278 explains this principle.
12. Goleman, as Chapter 1, note 6. Describes self-regulation: 'extreme displays of negative emotion have never emerged as a driver of good leadership'.
13. Graham Jones and Adrian Moorhouse, Developing Mental Toughness. Pages 11–28 describe pressure; page 40 describes mental toughness.
14. Goleman, Boyatzis and McKee, as Chapter 2, note 23. Page 7 describes mirroring, the attunement of emotions.
15. Kaplan, as Chapter 2, note 13. Explains creating a self-review.
16. Goffee and Jones, as Chapter 3, note 22. Describes how leaders reveal their weaknesses, arguing that 'sharing imperfection is so effective because it

underscores a human being's authenticity'.

17. Rick Lash, 'Top Leadership: Taking the Inner Journey', Ivy Business Journal, May/June, 2002.
18. Collins, as Chapter 2, note 2. Page 36 describes professional will and personal humility as the two sides of level 5 leadership.
19. Jim Collins, 'Level 5 Leadership: The Triumph of Humility and Fierce Resolve', Harvard Business Review, July–August, 2005.
20. Jones and Moorhouse, as above, note 13. Pages 79–108 describe how to stay strong in your self-belief.
21. Luft and Ingham, as Chapter 3, note 6.
22. Jones and Moorhouse, as above, note 13. Pages 112–14 explain the contrast between 'approach' and 'avoidance' motivation.
23. Dan Lovallo and Daniel Kahneman, 'Delusions of Success', Harvard Business Review, July, 2003.
24. Lovallo and Kahneman, as above, note 23 describes anchoring.
25. Lovallo and Kahneman, as above, note 23 puts optimism in its place.

Chapter 6. The Dark Side (Losing Behaviours)
1. Goleman, as Introduction, note 1.
2. Goleman, Boyatzis and McKee, as Chapter 2, note 23. Page 79 describes the impact of the style in the absence of emotional self-control.
3. Goleman, Boyatzis and McKee, as Chapter 2, note 23. Page 74 describes pacesetting.
4. Whitmore, as Chapter 4, note 1. Page 22 explores recall decline.
5. Jim Collins, as Chapter 2, note 27. Page 100 describes stage four of decline, grasping for salvation.
6. Goleman, Boyatzis and McKee, as Chapter 2, note 23. Page 5 describes the emotional task of a leader.
7. Spreier, Fontaine and Malloy, as Chapter 4, note 4 describes the destructive potential of overachievers.
8. LaFasto and Larson, as Chapter 2, note 4. Page 119 assesses high-control leaders.
9. Mark E Van Buren and Todd Safferstone, The Quick Wins Paradox. Describes problematic behaviours as new leaders go after early results.
10. Malcolm Gladwell, Outliers. Page 219 describes this approach as crucial.
11. Geert Hofstede, Cultural Dimensions Power Distance Index. One of a number of cultural indices; see www.geert-hofstede.com for definitions and raw scores.

Chapter 7, The Winning Feeling (Impact on Others)

1. Lencioni, as Chapter 2, note 7. Page 232 describes irrelevance.
2. Lencioni, as Chapter 2, note 7. Page 221 describes anonymity.
3. Kouzes and Posner, as Chapter 2, note 1. Page 30 characterises admired leaders.
4. O'Toole and Bennis, as Chapter 3, note 7. Describes rebuilding trust as a leader.
5. Horovitz with Ohlsson-Corboz, as Chapter 2, note 15. Page 157 describes the impact of trust with stretch and separately with support.
6. Luft and Ingham, as Chapter 3, note 6.
7. Simon Machin, 'The Nature of Internal Coaching Relationships', International Journal of Evidence Based Coaching and Mentoring, October, 2010, Special Issue No. 4. Pages 37–52 describe aspects of the coaching relationship.
8. Robert Galford and Anne Seibold Drapeau, 'The Enemies of Trust', Harvard Business Review, February, 2003. Explains why some people don't trust leaders.
9. Pink, as Chapter 4, note 2. Page 207 describes new forms of motivation and working.
10. W C H Prentice, 'Understanding Leadership', Harvard Business Review, January, 2004 (from an original article 1961). Describes a leader's focus on people's personal development.

Chapter 8. Getting Going

1. Greene and Grant, Solution Focused Coaching (adapted by Simon Machin).
2. Lash, as Chapter 5, note 17.

Chapter 9. Organisational Support

1. Mark Cook, UMIST, Research into recruitment and selection 1984.
2. Rob Ashmore, Involve: From a recruitment and selection toolkit created for Belron®.
3. Buckingham and Coffman, as Chapter 1, note 4. Pages 236–8 describe how to interview.
4. Machin, as Chapter 7, note 7. Appendix E proposes a coaching evaluation.

Chapter 10. Pulling It All Together

1. Lash, as Chapter 5, note 17.
2. Buckingham and Coffman, as Chapter 1, note 4. Page 21 describes the

measuring stick.

3. John Beeson, 'Why You Didn't Get That Promotion', Harvard Business Review, June, 2009. Describes how to decode the unwritten rules of career advancement.

4. Gobillot, as Chapter 2, note 14.

Appendices:

1. Goleman, as Introduction, note 1.

2. Kirsta Andersen and Guorong Zhu, Organizational Climate Survey. Technical Manual, Hay Group, August, 2002. Pages 5–6.

3. Goleman, Boyatzis and McKee, as Chapter 2, note 23. Pages 53–69 describe the resonant styles; pages 71–88 describe the dissonant styles.

4. Houldsworth and Machin, as Chapter 1, note 1.

5. Elizabeth Houldsworth and Dilum Jirasinghe, Managing and Measuring Employee Performance. Pages 169–76 describe an approach to leadership.

6. Emmanuel Gobillot, The Connected Leader. Pages 63–70 explain why leaders are valued by followers.

INDEX

Page references in *italic* indicate Figures and diagnostics.